Louis Hamilton
12th July '05

Roger Büdeler

Pyrenees 3

Eastern Spanish Pyrenees: Val d'Aran to Núria (with Andorra)

Translated by Gill Round

50 selected valley and high mountain walks
in the Eastern Spanish Pyrenees

With 85 colour photos,
50 small walking maps to a scale of 1:25,000 / 1:50,000 / 1:75,000 and
2 overview maps to a scale of 1:550,000 and 1:850,000

ROTHER · MUNICH

Cover Foto:
Circ dels Pessons (Andorra)

Frontispiece (page 2):
Vall de Gerber

All photos by the author

Cartography:
walking maps to a scale of 1: 25,000 / 1:50,000 /1:75,000
Kartografie Christian Rolle, Holzkirchen
Overview maps to a scale of 1: 500,000 and 1:850,000
© Freytag & Berndt, Vienna

Translation:
Gill Round

The descriptions of all the walks given in this guide are made according to the best knowledge of the authors. The use of this guide is at one's own risk. As far as is legally permitted, no responsibility will be accepted for possible accidents, damage or injury of any kind.

1st edition 2005
© Bergverlag Rother GmbH, Munich

ISBN 3-7633-4828-X

Distributed in Great Britain by Cordee, 3a De Montfort Street, Leicester
Great Britain LE1 7HD, www.cordee.co.uk

ROTHER WALKING GUIDES

Algarve · Andalusia South · Azores · Bernese Oberland East · Corsica · Côte d'Azur · Crete East · Crete West · Cyprus · Gomera · Gran Canaria · Iceland · La Palma · Madeira · Mallorca · Mont Blanc · Norway South · Provence · Pyrenees 1, 2, 3 · Sardinia · Sicily · High Tatra · Tenerife · Tuscany North · Valais East · Valais West · Vanoise · Around the Zugspitze

Dear mountain lovers! We would be happy to hear your opinion and suggestions for amendment to this Rother walking guide.

BERGVERLAG ROTHER · Munich
D-85521 Ottobrunn · Haidgraben 3 · Tel. (089) 608669-0, Fax -69
Internet www.rother.de · **E-mail** bergverlag@rother.de

Foreword

The eastern Spanish Pyrenees are not a homogenous mountain region with a rigid boundary line. Within the superficial regional border there are many hidden independent mountain and valley landscapes with a large and contrasting richness of forms. Jagged granite towers above glistening lakes, steep limestone rock faces topped with karstic ridges and pyramids of red-coloured slate amidst green pastures. These are just some of the features of the diverse mountain landscapes which you can only appreciate in all their nuances when you are on a walk.

A prominent attraction of the eastern Spanish Pyrenees is the Aigüestortes i Estany de St. Maurici national park which has many visitors each year. Its distinctive and fascinating scenery is characterised by countless picturesque mountain lakes and idyllic small valleys against a backdrop of sheer rock buttresses and filigreed mountain ridges and peaks. You cannot fail to be enchanted if you venture off the beaten track from the two or three main routes and hike into some of the quieter side-valleys, ascend over a high pass from one delightful area of lakes to another or climb an unfrequented summit. But the national park is only one part of this hiking area's complex mosaic. The Sierra de Cadí is no less impressive where the seemingly impenetrable steep crags rise up out of green meadows and wooded slopes to form soft peaks; or the remote Vall de Ferrera with the staggeringly beautiful massif of Pica d'Estats ... and lastly Andorra, where – away from the hustle and bustle of the central valley – you can hike through wonderful havens with valleys full of beautiful flowers and captivating lakes amongst spectacular mountain scenery.

Volume 3 of the Pyrenees walking guide links with the central Spanish Pyrenees. It starts with Val d'Aran and follows the main Pyrenean ridge, including the separate Sierra de Cadí, to Vall de Núria whose mountains approach the 3000m mark. The Pyrenees further east drop down abruptly to the level of the lower Pyrenees and, in the high ranges of Alberas, eventually display a distinctly Mediterranean character.

There's a good network of paths for the intrepid hiker which includes the famous GR11 and its alternatives as well as the more challenging Pyrenean high mountain trail. There are also many local paths offering delightful opportunities for combining local culture and scenery.

Spring 2005   Roger Büdeler

Contents

Foreword 5
Tourist tips 8
Walking in the eastern Spanish Pyrenees 16
    Outdoor sport in the Catalonian Pyrenees 19
Information and addresses from A-Z 20
    Overview map 22

Val d'Aran 24
  1 Circ dera Artiga 26
  2 Refugi dera Restanca, 2010m, and Lac de Mar, 2235m 28
  3 Montardo d'Aran, 2833m 30
  4 Refugi de Colomèrs, 2098m, and Lac Obago, 2221m 32
  5 Long circular walk through the Circ de Colomèrs 34
  6 Lacs de Baciver, 2320m 36
  7 Tuc de Pèdescauç, 2416m 38
  8 Vall de Gerber 42
  9 Pic d'Amitges, 2851m 44

Parc Nacional d'Aigüestortes
i Estany de St. Maurici 48
  10 Planell d'Aigüestortes, 1820m 50
  11 Portarró d'Espot, 2424m 52
  12 Refugi Ventosa i Calvell, 2242m 54
  13 Vall Fosca and its lakes 56
  14 Walk around the Estany de St. Maurici, 1915m 58
  15 Estany Negre de Peguera, 2330m 60
  16 Through the Vall de Monestero 62
  17 Pic de Monestero, 2878m 64
  18 Vall and Pic de Subenuix, 2949m 66
  19 Pòrt de Ratera, 2580m, and Tuc de Ratera, 2862m 70
  20 Refugi d'Amitges, 2380m 74
  21 Estany de la Gola, 2249m 76

Vall de Cardós and Vall de Ferrera 78
  22 Estany del Diable, 2320m, and Pic de Campirme, 2633m 80
  23 Estanys de Sottlo, 2345m, and d'Estats, 2465m 82
  24 Port de Boet, 2509m 84
  25 Estanys de Baiau, 2480m 86
  26 Ermita St. Miquel, 1200m, and Besan, 1160m 88

Andorra 90
27 Refugi de Coma Pedrosa, 2272m, and Pic de Coma Pedrosa,
   2942m 92
28 Through the Circ de Tristaina, 2500m 94
29 Pic de Tristaina, 2878m 96
30 Estany Blau, 2335m 98
31 Vall de Sorteny and Pic de la Serrera, 2913m 100
32 Estany de l'Estanyó, 2340m 102
33 Pic de Casamanya, 2740m 104
34 Estanys de Juclar, 2294m, and Coll de l'Alba, 2546m 106
35 Circ dels Pessons and Pic de Gargantillar, 2864m 110
36 Vall de Madriu 114

**Parc Natural Cadí-Moixeró
and upper Cerdanya** 116
37 Vall de la Llosa 118
38 Puigpedrós, 2914m 120
39 Estanys de Malniu, 2310m 122
40 Circular walk at the foot of the Sierra de Cadí 124
41 Prat de Cadí, 1820m 126
42 Refugi Prat d'Aguiló (Cèsar August Torras), 2037m 128
43 Comabona, 2547m 130
44 Penyes Altes de Moixeró, 2276m 132
45 Vulturó, 2638m 134
46 Pedraforca, 2497m 136

Vall de Núria 138
47 Puigmal, 2913m 140
48 Along the Camí Vell from Queralbs to Núria 144
49 Through the Gorgues del Freser and along the Camí dels
   Enginyers 148
50 Pic de Noufonts, 2861m 152

Index 156
Catalan – English glossary for mountain walkers 159

Tourist tips

Use of this guide
The hiking area of the eastern Spanish Pyrenees is identical to the Pyrenees in the province of Catalonia. It covers Val d'Aran, the adjoining southeastern national park of Aigüestortes i Estany de St.Maurici, Vall de Cardós and Vall Ferrera, the Cerdanya mountain region of the independent natural park of Sierra de Cadí-Moixeró as well as the mountain regions around Núria in the province of Ripoll which forms the geographical border in the east. Andorra is also included but, although an independent state, it still belongs to the central ridge of the Pyrenees.

Albera, on the other hand, is the chain of mountains which runs down to the Mediterranean and has been separated off to be included in the Costa Brava walking guide.

Every walk description is introduced by an information section which contains the most important details and tips needed to plan and carry out a walk. A characterisation of the walk is followed by a description of the route. This is kept short and to the point, especially where the paths are clear and appropriately waymarked. The approximate line of the route is marked in colour on the little walking map which should in no way replace a detailed walking map.

An overview map (p. 22/23) shows the geographical location of all the walks.

Grade
Judging the difficulty of a mountain walk can be quite tricky. The various requirements of the hiker as well as the conditions that prevail on the day of a walk (weather, state of paths etc.) often make an objective assessment of the technical and fitness demands problematic. A few metres of scrambling up rock might be child's play to some, but a real climbing challenge to others.

The same can be said of exposed paths, steep scree slopes or exposed summits. The grade levels, therefore, only give an approximate indication of the challenges you may expect. In the information section and/or walk description, special mention is made of sections where some climbing is involved, or there's a danger of landslides or an area of steep ascent. In each case the hiker must be responsible for assessing what he/she is capable of. Grades of difficulty relate to the specified destination. Sections of the route, for example, like a walk through a valley or over a pass before ascending the summit, can be much easier; alternatively, the length of a walk or an additional summit ascent may increase the grade of the walk. Your attention is drawn to this in the alternatives described in the introductory information section.

BLUE
Easy walks with no risks attached on clear paths which are, for the most part, well marked. The length of time needed for the walk is within certain limits. Gradients are moderate, but some short steeper sections may be included. Larger variations in height are spread over a longer distance.

RED
Moderately difficult routes which demand a greater degree of energy and fitness due to their length as well as their steeper and more persistent gradients. Paths may run across precipitous terrain or be slightly exposed and may include a bit of scrambling. Walking and climbing over boulders is also possible. Experience of walking in mountains is required as well as sure-footedness and a sense of direction.

BLACK
Difficult, long walks demanding a good level of fitness which go through high mountain areas and onto summits. They are recommended only for experienced and trained mountain walkers. Together with big height variations, strenuous and steep gradients and exposed areas there may also be short sections where some climbing is necessary (grade II maximum).

Paths
Most of the hiking paths in this guide are well constructed and maintained.

'Black' terrain: steep scree slope up to Pic de Subenuix (Walk 18).

Signposts will often guide you to the starting points and give directions at important junctions. GR paths (Gran Recorrido) and their alternatives are waymarked throughout in white and red; PRC paths (Pequeño Recorrido de Catalunya) are waymarked as a rule in yellow or white and yellow.

Dangers

Summit ascents and walks in the high mountains occasionally go over difficult terrain where you can expect to find exposed paths, boulder fields and steep scree slopes. Sure-footedness and experience are therefore essential. The crossing of mountain streams without a bridge can be tricky especially during snow melt. Slippery and wobbly stones and rocks, as well as wood when it's wet, are also sources of danger; if in doubt you should go across in bare feet, providing the depth of the water and current allow for this.

A sudden change in the weather with a marked drop in temperature, snow, fog and strong winds are also not unknown in the sunny south of the Pyrenees and require the relevant protective clothing and equipment. Due to their location and altitude some isolated mountain chains and massifs like the Sierra de Cadí or the national park of Aigües Tortes y Sant Maurici are sometimes favourite focal points for the regular summer afternoon thunder-

A storm brewing above Pedraforca (Walk 46).

storms. Careful planning of the walk, checking weather information and an early start are the best way to safeguard against dangerous surprises.

Equipment

Standard hiking gear – sturdy footwear and practical clothing – is essential on all of the walks. Take clothing that is comfortable enough when it's hot and at the same time, gives you sufficient protection against rain, cold and wind. It's advisable to take a good supply of sun protection with you in the summer. Walking poles are a great help over steep scree-covered terrain, and also for crossing streams. It is particularly important to take enough fluids and food with you, especially on long walks and in the high mountains, even if there's a staffed hut along the way. Maps are not only useful for checking directions during your walk, they can also help you identify the surrounding peaks and valleys.

Maps

The best topographical maps available are to a scale of 1:25,000 from the Institut Cartogràfic de Catalunya, but only the important or officially waymarked hiking paths are marked. Walking maps designed for the hiker are also published by the cartographic institute of Catalonia in the 'mapa excursionista. PIRINEUS' series (1:50,000). They form an altogether reliable basis for the walks in this guide. They are covered in the following editions:
– Walks 1-26: Pica d'Estats-Aneto (no. 22). Walk 26 is also available in the map Pica d'Estats-Mont Roig by Ed. Alpina (1:25,000).
– Walks 25 and 27-46: ANDORRA-CADÍ (no. 21).
– Walks 47-50: PUIGMAL-COSTABONA (no. 20)

For the Parc Nacional d'Aigüestortes i Estany de Sant Maurici a special map is recommended by the Institut Cartogràfic de Catalunya in the series 'Espais naturals protegits' no. 01 to a scale of 1:25,000.

Walking times

The time details given represent real walking time at a moderate pace and do not include breaks or other stops. The actual length of time taken depends, of course, on one's individual walking speed and fitness and there not being any unforeseen complications.

Refugis (Mountain huts)

There are numerous huts well situated in this hiking area which are, for the most part, looked after by the Catalonian mountaineering organisations. They are usually open and staffed in the summer months from June to September, but only at the weekends in May and October depending on the snow and weather conditions. Since most of the huts are very full in the high season, you should always book ahead for an overnight stay.

Outside the summer season the hiker will usually find a modest number of overnight places available in the unstaffed huts.

Metal bivouac in Vall de Gerber (Walk 8).

The refuges (or custodians) mentioned in the guide are contactable on the following telephone numbers (number of places in brackets):

■ Val d'Aran
- Ref. Restanca (80) ✆ 608.03 65 59 (www.restanca.com)
- Ref. de Colomèrs (40) ✆ 973. 25 30 08 / 973. 64 05 92 (open all year)
- Ref. de Saborèdo (21) ✆ 973.25 30 15 / 973.25 24 63

■ Parque Nacional d'Aigües Tortes y Estany de St.Maurici
- Ref. Ventosa i Calvell (80) ✆ 973.29 70 90 / 973.64 18 09 (www.refugiventosa.com)
- Ref. d'Amitges (66) ✆ 973.25 01 09 / 973.25 00 07 (www.amitges.com)
- Ref. Ernest Mallafré (24) ✆ 973.25 01 18 / 973.25 01 0
- Ref. J. M. Blanc (40) ✆ 973.25 01 08 / 93.423 23 45 (www.refugijmblanc.com
- Ref. Colomina (40) ✆ 973.25 20 00 / 973.68 10 42 (www.casulleras.com/colomina
- Ref. d'Estany Llong (49) ✆ 00882.16 50 10 00 90 / 629.37 46 52

■ Vall Cardós and Vall Ferrera
- Ref. de la Pleta del Prat (60) ✆ 973.62 30 79 / 973.62 30 89
- Ref. de Vallferrera (21) ✆ 973.62 43 78 / 973.62 07 54

■ Andorra
- Ref. de Comapedrosa (60) ✆ 376.32 79 55 / 376. 73 69 00

■ Cerdanya and Naturpark 'Sierra de Cadí-Moixeró'
- Ref. de Malniu (26) ✆ 93.825 71 04 / 616.85 55 35 (www.guiesmeranges.com)
- Ref. de Prat d'Aguiló (38) ✆ 973.25 01 35 / 639.71 40 87
- Refugi Lluís Estasèn ✆ 608315312

■ Vall de Núria
- Ref. de Coma de Vaca ('Manelic') (20) ✆ 972.19 80 82 / 93.682 42.37 (www.comadevaca.com)

The tourist offices provide up-to-date information.
Detailed information about all the staffed and unstaffed huts and, in each case, the choice of walks and summit ascents, is given in the hut guide 'Refugios Pirenaicos', PRAMES S.A., Zaragoza w.y.

Getting there
For most of the walks you cannot do without your own car. There is only a bus service in the larger towns in the main valleys and even then, it's a very limited service. Smaller mountain valleys are often connected to the main valleys by good roads, although the actual starting points of the walks are sometimes only accessible along lengthy tracks or roadways of varying standards. Roadways described here are usually driveable in a normal car with due care and respect. If you prefer a more comfortable drive you can hire a 4x4 taxi to take you to the starting point and then arrange to be collected at the end. Information about taxis is obtainable from the tourist offices and you will sometimes find notices up in bars in the area.

Refugi Colomina (Walk 13).

■ Aigüestortes i Estany de Sant Maurici national park

Access into the national park and certain border areas is generally forbidden. There's a regular 4x4 taxi service:
- Aigüestortes region: goes from Boí (village square), ✆ 973.69 63 14. Taxi service as far as Aigüestortes.
- Estany de St. Maurici-Region: goes from Espot (Ortseingang), ✆ 973.62 41 05, as far as Estany de St. Maurici, Refugi d'Amitges and Estany Tort de Peguera.
- Refugi Restanca: goes from Punt deth Ressèc as far as Pontet de Rius.
- Refugi Colomèrs: goes from the mandatory car park at Bahns de Tredòs as far as the refuge hiking path.

■ Vall de Núria

There's a cog railway on the stretch Ribes de Freser – Queralbs – Santuari de Núria (Cremallera) ✆ 93.205 15 15. Journey time in each direction is 50 minutes.

Protection of nature
Please be aware of the general code of conduct on every walk and support the protection of the mountains. There are special regulations in the Aigüestortes i Estany de Sant Maurici and in the Parc Natural de Sierra de Cadí-Moixeró. Information boards along the hiking paths and at the park

boundaries give you details of the individual regulations. The tourist offices also have information brochures available.

Long distance paths

The GR11 running between the Mediterranean and the Atlantic in the Spanish Pyrenees (Sendero de Gran Recorrido) is, for the most part, well constructed and maintained. With an ideal combination of valley and high mountain trails it crosses the most scenically beautiful areas and neighbourhoods mostly in the foothills of the main Pyrenean ridge. The individual stages of the walk are calculated in such a way that either a hut or some other accommodation is easily reached. The GR11 is suitable only for experienced mountain walkers and, under normal conditions in summer, does not require any special equipment such as crampons or ice axes. Sections of the path usually only lead up to moderate altitudes and very rarely onto a summit, which means that the GR11 or individual sections of it can be walked from early to late in the season. The numerous variations of the long distance path can also be very interesting and enable you to explore an area more intensely.

The ARP (Alta Ruta Pirenaica) – in the French Pyrenees HRP (Haute Randonnée Pyrénéenne) – is an attractive high mountain trail which runs on both sides of the central massif and is suitable only for skilled mountain hikers. It includes some sections of pathless and exposed terrain up to heights of just under 3000m.

Tips for long distance walkers

Thanks to a good network of paths, multi-day walks over passes and through valleys can be combined in various ways.

The scenically beautiful hut-to-hut walks in the Aigüestortes i Estany de Sant Maurici national park are well known. The third edition of the map Carros de Foc (www.carrosdefoc.com), just published, shows the classic circular hut walk through the national park. The numerous hiking trails make it possible to vary the walk as you wish. It's also worth mentioning the plethora of huts in Andorra which enables you to plan a variety of pleasant long distance walks. Although all the huts are unstaffed, except for the Refugi de Comapedrosa, they are reliable and comfortable.

Estany Trullo with the mountains of Val d'Aran in the background (Walk 15).

Walking in the eastern Spanish Pyrenees

Geography
It's difficult to distinguish the eastern Spanish Pyrenees from the central massif. This walking guide encompasses the Pyrenees lying in the province of Catalonia which begin to the east of the huge Maladata massif with Val D'Aran extending far northwards. Adjoining in the south is the Aigüestortes i Estany de St. Maurici national park which runs along the central ridge of the Pyrenees. To the east of the Río Noguera Pallaresa, the dead end valleys of Cardós and Ferrera branch off with the massif of Pica d'Estats which, at 3143m, forms the highest peak of the Catalonian mountain chain. The principality of Andorra occupies a special position politically, but its mountains belong to the central Pyrenean axis. Geologically of younger origin is the Sierra de Cadí which begins in the south of Andorra and is separated from the central ridge by a tectonic U-shaped valley between Seu d'Urgell and Puigcerda. On the other side of the large valley basin of Puigcerda and Font-Romeu the Pyrenees rise up around Vall de Núria to just under the 3000m mark and after Pic de Costabona suddenly drop down to a moderate level. The mountains here have already lost their high alpine character.

Vegetation
A really diverse vegetation is dominant in the remote mountain regions which is in keeping with the alignment of the valleys and the altitude of the mountains. Scots pines, uncinate pines and firs are the main representatives of conifers; beech and oak are predominant amongst the deciduous trees, sometimes the common maple too. Amongst the undergrowth you will find box tree, juniper, bilberry, heather and cistus which is often widespread in the granite areas. The diversity and sometimes density of flowers is enormous and can only be touched upon here. Together with endemic species like ramonda you will find crocus, Turk's cap lily and dog's tooth violet, Pyrenean buttercup, arnika, monkshood, white narcissus, foxglove, Pyrenean valerian and diverse species of gentians, cowslips and saxiphrage. The protected Vall de

Dwarf mountain pine in Vall de Subenuix.

Sorteny in the Ordino valley in Andorra is unique with regard to the diversity of flowers. Over a hundred different species grow in this relatively small valley region and they cover the hillsides with a carpet of multi-coloured flowers.

Fauna

Typically Mediterranean species of animals are not often found in the Catalonian Pyrenees. Amongst the mammals, the chamoix is quite widespread in the high mountain areas together with marmots too. Deer are rare, but are slowly on the increase. In many of the forests you might be lucky enough to come across pine martens. The Pyrenean mountain salamander is endemic amongst the amphibians. Reptiles are represented by the yellow and green viper, occasionally the asp viper too, and various types of lizards. In the numerous stretches of water which are, however, often short of nutrients you will find wild trout, barbel and carp. Species of birds are on the other hand quite diverse. Griffon vultures and lammergeyers are prevalent amongst those birds of prey that are able to find ideal living conditions on steep rock faces and in deep valleys, as well as the golden eagle and the short-toed eagle. From the broad palette of other bird species it's worth mentioning grouse and partridge, wall creeper, ring ouzel, dipper, crossbill, rock thrush, citril finch, both the loud alpine chough and larger chough and last but not least, very rare in the rest of Spain, the black woodpecker which has been made into the symbol of the Cadí-Moixeró nature park.

National park und nature reserves

The Parc Nacional d'Aigüestortes i Estany de St. Maurici was established in 1955 over a surface area of more than 10,000 hectares. Today it forms the protected central region which is surrounded by a border area (zona perifèrica) with graded levels of protection such as access restrictions. A deciding factor in the setting up of the national park was the presence of glaciation features in the region. The polished granite formations, the eroded U-shaped valleys and especially the numerous lakes lying at high altitude can be explored and studied throughout the hiking area. These lakes, which vary greatly in depth and size, were formed in the ice-age during the course of which, basins were carved out and then filled up with water from the melting glaciers. The valleys of Riu de St. Nicolau in the west and Riu Escrita in the east, connected by the pass of Portarró d'Espot, have for a long time presented the easiest approach into the mountains which are sealed off by high and precipitous ranges. Today they also offer the mostly used and regulated access for walks in the national park.

Sign at the entrance to the national park.

The Cadí-Moixeró natural park was founded in 1983 over a surface area of more than 41,000 hectares. In its present extent it includes the Sierra de Cadí, the Sierra de Moixeró, the Pedraforca massif as well as parts of the Tosa d'Alp and Puigllançada massifs. There are special regulations for the protection of nature in the natural park and conditions of use which, with regard to the forest economy, for example, contributed to the conservation of beautiful forest areas on the north side of the Sierra de Cadí. The mountains were created in a geologically younger age than the Pyrenean central ridge and are separated from it, also geographically, by a pronounced mountain basin. What is striking, is the sharp contrast between the steeply falling limestone slopes of the north wall and the rather more gentle gradients of the southern slopes. This is particularly noticeable in the narrower region of the Sierra de Cadí.

Parc Nacional d'Aigüestortes i Estany de St. Maurici
The national park offers two central information offices in Boí and Espot together with other smaller information points.
Opening times: 9.00-13.00 and 15.30-19.00 (daily from 1.April to 31.October)
Casa del Parc Nacional de Boí: Plaça del Treio, 3; 25528 Boí. ✆ 973.696189
Casa del Parc Nacional d'Espot: Prat del Guarda, 4; 25597 Espot. ✆ 973.624036
Internet: www.parcsdecatalunya.net/aiguestortes.htm

Parc Natural Cadí-Moixeró
The information office of the park authorities can be found in Bagà: Carrer de la Vinya, 1; 08695 Bagà. ✆ 93.8244151.
Opening times: 9.00-13.30 and 15.30-18.30 (weekdays). Limited opening times on Saturdays and Sundays.
There are also local information points in Bellver de Cerdanya (town hall, Plaça de Sant Roc ✆ 973.510016) and Tuixén (town hall) ✆ 973.370030.
Internet: www.parcsdecatalunya.net/cadi.htm

OUTDOOR SPORT IN THE CATALONIAN PYRENEES

Canyoning

There are numerous opportunities for practising this mountain water sport. The most beautiful gorges are to be found in the pre-Pyrenean regions, amongst them

the classics like Barranc de l'Infern, Viu de Llevata, Gorgas de Gavarra, Gorga de St.Aniol and Gorgas de Núria. In the towns and villages in the larger valleys there are countless organisations for guided walks.

Route descriptions can be found in the German guide by Roger Büdeler / Gabriele Flitner: Die schönsten Canyoningtouren in den Pyrenäen und Sierra de Guara, Bergverlag Rother, 1997 (available only in German).

Climbing

Attractive climbing routes up to the highest grade can be found in all of the regions, in the central mountains and the limestone dominated pre-Pyrenees which frequently offer superb rock faces. Especially challenging are the jagged Agulles which are divided by steep clefts in the Aigüestortes i Estany de St. Maurici national park. Also well known to climbers are the Roques de Totlomón in Vall de Núria. Via ferrata are less widespread. Mountain guides are available in the resort and from tourist offices.

Cycling and mountain biking (VTT)

Several passes in the foothills of the Pyrenees are favourite goals for competition cyclists, amongst them the Coll del Cantó between Sort and La Seu d'Urgell. A severe test is the famous high mountain pass of Port de la Bonaigua which connects Val d'Aran and Pallars Sobirá. Many forest tracks and roadways allow scenic mountain bike tours. The tourist offices frequently have route plans available for mountain biking.

Skiing and snow-shoeing

Andorra is the centre for skiing and snow-shoeing. There are ski centres in almost all areas with large lift systems and numerous prepared slopes. Outside of Andorra there are rather more modest possibilities. Super-Espot at the edge of the Sierra de Cadí national park, Baqueira-Beret in Val d'Aran and Super-Molina at the northwestern edge are worth mentioning.

Ski tour enthusiasts will find fantastic opportunities in the most beautiful mountain scenery including lovely summit walks. The same applies to the increasingly popular sport of snow-shoeing which is possible on many routes in this guide.

Wild water rafting

Kayaking and rafting are very popular and widespread in the Catalonian Pyrenees. The Río Noguera Pallaresa south of Llavorsí is the most frequented river and is even specially regulated for the purpose.

Both the little villlages of Sort and Llavorsí are centres for this much sought-after watersport.

Information and addresses from A-Z

Information
General tourist offices:
Torisme Val d'Aran : Ctra. De Gausach, 1 ; 25530 Vielha. ℂ 973.640688.
torisme@aran.org / www.aran.org
Patronat de Turisme de Terres de Lleida : Rambla Ferran, 18 ; 25007 Lleida.
ℂ 973.245408.
lleidatur@lleidatur.es / www.lleidatur.es
Sindicat d'Iniciativa-Oficina de Turisme: C/Doctor Vilanova, s/n; Andorra la Vella. ℂ (376).820214.
sindicatdiniciativa@andorra.ad / www.turisme.ad
Patronat de Turisme Costa Brava Girona: Emil Grahit, 13-15; 17002 Girona.
ℂ 972.208401.
costabrava@costabrava.org / www.costabrava.org

Try www.rother.de (WebLinks/GeoLinks) for many useful links.

Mountain rescue
For emergencies telephone ℂ 112. Otherwise on hand: Bombers (fire service) ℂ 085 (Andorra: ℂ 118) and Mossos d'Esquadra (police) ℂ 088 (Andorra: ℂ 110)

Camping und wild camping
Campsites of varying standards are numerous and usually open from June to September, some also all year round.
Camping is generally forbidden in the Parc Nacional d'Aigüestortes i Estany de St. Maurici, and only permitted in certain areas in the Parc Natural Sierra de Cadí-Moixeró and with the permission of the relevant regional authority.

National holidays and festivals
The main holiday period in summer climaxes in the month of August at which time you can expect the campsites and staffed mountain huts to be fully occupied. Next to that, Easter (Semana Santa) is a traditional holiday week.
There are village fiestas for as many reasons as there are grains of sand at the seaside. Every village and every town organises their own fiesta with food, music and dancing. A relevant calendar of events is available from the tourist offices.

Opening times
Shops are usually open Monday to Saturday between 10.00 and 14.00 and 17.00 and 20. Bakeries tend to be open on a Sunday morning as well.

Vall de Sorteny (Walk 31): an enchanting garden of flowers.

Time to travel
Because of their warm temperatures and settled weather conditions, May and June are very pleasant months for hiking, as well as September and October. Depending on the duration and intensity of the snow showers during winter you can expect to come across areas of snow in certain high and exposed areas in early summer. In high summer the climate is hot from the middle of July and in August. Late summer frequently has stable weather conditions with settled temperatures, but from the second half of October the weather can be very changeable with autumn rain and the first falls of snow at high altitude. November and December can also be really mild before the actual winter begins with heavy snowfalls and low temperatures.

Telephone:
Dialling code for Spain 0034; Andorra 00376.

Hiking and mountaineering clubs:
FEEC (Federació d'Entitats Excursionistes de Catalunya) ✆ 93.4120777
www.feec.es
CEC (Centre Excursionista de Catalunya) ✆ 93 3152311
Federació Andorrana de Muntanyisme ✆ (376) 867444

Weather forecasts
Tourist offices are the best source of official weather forecasts. Telephone information can be obtained from the Instituto Nacional de Meteorologia ✆ 906.365325; in Andorra ✆ 848852.

Val d'Aran

As blue as the sea: Lac de Mar (Walk 2).

Situated in the north of the highest Pyrenean massif, Val d'Aran was for a long time bordered by its neighbouring Spanish provinces. A connection to the neighbouring eastern region of Pallars Sobirà did exist above the over 2000m high Port de la Bonaigua, but the southern approach from the Río Noguera Ribagorçana valley caused a great deal of difficulty. The crossing of the high rock barrier, narrow as it is, between the massifs of Maladeta and Besiberri was complicated even in summer, and therefore in winter completely impossible. The isolated position of Val d'Aran meant that the local language and customs held out for a long time.

It was not until the building of the Vielha tunnel that Val d'Aran was liberated from its geographical separation and was able to develop into one of the most popular walking areas in the Spanish Pyrenees. Practically encircled by high mountain ranges which are only broken through effectively by the valley of Río Garona on the border with France, Val d'Aran offers a plethora of walks for all tastes. There's a wide range from high mountain walks onto summits of the mighty Besiberri massif to walks through unspoiled narrow valleys like that of the Río Torán in whose dense woods you can easily get lost. It is the mountain basin of glacial origin, of course, in the northern border zone of the Parc Nacional d'Aigüestortes i Estany de St. Maurici with its fantastic accumulation of mountain lakes, which is a firm favourite with tourists.

The impressive Circs around the huts of Restanca, Colomèrs and Saborèdo are easily accessible from Artiés, Salardú and Tredòs through the valleys which penetrate to the south, whereby a multitude of day walks and summit ascents – Montardo d'Aran! – can be realised without any great effort. At the same time, for long distance walkers, there are some most beautiful approaches into the central area of the national park.

A look at the map of Val d'Aran shows that winter tourism is thought of as important even here. However, the ski lifts and slopes of Baqueira-Beret in the east of the region are the only provision for this which is currently worth mentioning and even they do not really spoil the beautiful mountain surroundings of the Marimanha massif. Only a few paces away you are walking beside mountain streams through unspoiled grassy hillsides up to azure blue lakes or onto surprising ridge tops with spectacular views. The view of the Maladeta massif with Pico de Aneto is nowhere as impressive as from the hills and mountains around the Plan de Beret! The high wide valley, in the summer a cattle pasture, is also a starting point for an extremely popular walk through the valley where the Río Noguera Pallaresa originates. Some objectives are the Santuari de Montgarri and the deserted hamlet of the same name which became widely famous through the fate of its inhabitants who held out to the last.

On the way to Montardo d'Aran (Walk 3).

Similarly popular, even if for other reasons, is the valley of Artiga de Lin in the southwest of Val d'Aran. This is where, in the impressive waterfall of Uelhs deth Joèu – literally the eyes of Jupiter – those melt waters of Pico de Aneto, which flow underground in the Forau dels Aiguallats, reach daylight again. According to a persistent legend it's supposed to be the actual source of the Río Garona, later called the Garonne.

1 Circ dera Artiga

Short circular walk in the Artiga-de-Lin valley

Uelhs deth Joèu – Plan dera Artiga de Lin – Uelhs deth Joèu

Location: Es Bòrdes, 860m.
Starting point: car park near to Uelhs deth Joèu, 1390m. In Es Bòrdes follow the signs for Artiga de Lin 7.7km to the signposted car park.

Walking times: total time 1¼ hrs.
Height difference: 90m.
Grade: easy stroll.
Refreshments: no eating places along the way; Es Bòrdes.

Only a few pretty huts adorn the green Val dera Artiga de Lin west of Vielha. The long valley is a popular destination for a day out and is an enchanting natural attraction. The legendary waterfall of Uelhs deth Joèu spews out the glacier waters of the Aneto massif again which disappear in the Forau dels Aigualluts in a cave and the superb mountain basin at the head of the valley creates an impressive background for this leisurely walk. Stone benches, tables and a barbecue provide an inviting place for a picnic under the shade of trees.

You can already hear the mighty roar of the imposing Uelhs deth Joèu waterfall in the **car park**. A sign indicates your path and after only a few minutes you reach the water cascading down over broad ledges. A metal bridge brings you over to the other side of the mountain stream and you ascend steeply up through the pretty mixed wood and moss covered rocks. Little steps have sometimes been built into the path. The path levels out af-

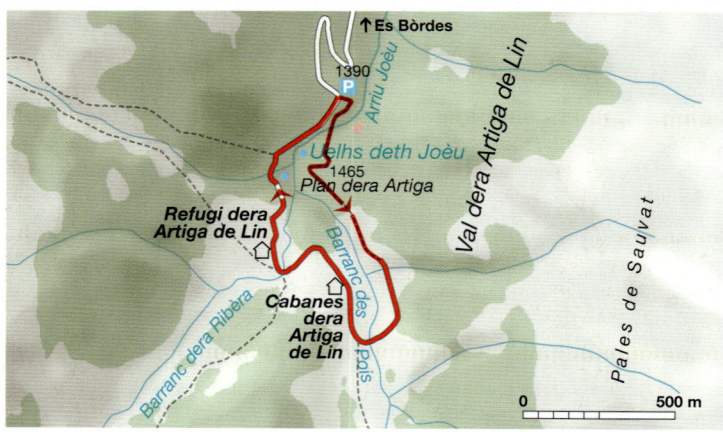

ter a stone gateway and is lined with tall grasses and flowers amongst which you will find some quite rare species. At a second stone portal the wood comes to an end and you enter the **Plan dera Artiga de Lin**, 1465m, a valley arena enclosed by high mountains. Walk along the old roadway in the bottom of the valley, cross over the Barranc des Pois which drops steeply down from a lake lying 600m higher and you come to a shepherd's hut on the left of the path. Beyond this a circle of mountains of smaller dimensions opens out. A little bridge leads you over the Barranc dera Ribera and a little further on you have reached the Refugi dera Artiga de Lin. From here the white and yellow marked hiking path climbs up to the Port dera Picada, a connecting pass between Val d'Aran and the Benasque valley. From the refuge take the asphalt track and after a few minutes you arrive back at the car park.

The cascades of Uelhs deth Joèu.

One of the typical huts in the Artiga valley.

2 Refugi dera Restanca, 2010m, and Lac de Mar, 2235m

A dream of a lake!

Pònt deth Ressèc – Refugi dera Restanca – Lac de Mar and back

Location: Artíes, 1140m.
Starting point: car park at the Pònt deth Ressèc, 1395m. From Artíes (signposted 'Restanca') go along an asphalt track as far as the mandatory car park with information board.
Walking times: Pònt deth Ressèc - Refugi dera Restanca 1¾ hrs.; Refugi dera Restanca – Lac de Mar 1 hr; return 2½ hrs.; total time 5¼ hrs..
Height difference: 840m.
Grade: technically straightforward walk with some steeper inclines. GR as far as the refuge, white and yellow marked path from there to the lake.
Refreshments: Ref. d. Restanca; Artíes.
Tip: there's a 4x4 taxi service from the Pont deth Ressèc to the Pontet de Rius (see page 13).
Alternative: Lac de Mar – Colhada de Lac de Mar – Lac Tòrt de Rius – Lac de Rius – Refugi dera Restanca. This varied circular walk requires a good degree of fitness and takes you over a very steep pass and through two neighbouring valleys. Total time there and back from the Pont deth Ressèc 8 to 9 hrs. with a height variation of about 1200m. At the southern tip of the Lac de Mar the path continues directly onto the southeastern slope of the Grinches de Rius. It twists and turns uphill really steeply and then goes round lengthy bends up to a very steep section where some bits of scrambling are needed. After that the gradient decreases up onto the **Colhada de Lac de Mar**, 2510m: fantastic view down onto the basin of lakes of the neighbouring valley, Montardo d'Aran and Besiberri. The path to this mass of lakes descends relatively moderately. It is marked with numerous cairns and keeps to the right of, and at some distance away from, both the multi-armed first lake and the large **Lac Tòrt de Rius**, 2350m, later on. With some ups-and-downs it leads through the most beautiful granite landscape and eventually approaches **Lac de Rius**, 2320m. At the eastern edge of this lake it meets the GR11, turns right here to go out of the valley through the at first dry Rius valley strewn with large boulders which is bordered in the north by precipitously steep and eroded rock faces. The valley gradually becomes greener and broader and the path continues to keep on the right hand slope of the valley across undulating pastureland and then ascends a little before descending quickly into a hardly perceptible side-valley. Ascending suddenly again on the opposite hillside and steeply near some electricity pylons you reach the dam wall of Restanca lake.

Lac de Mar (see photo on page 24) – a really unusual name for a mountain lake lying at an altitude of over 2200m. However everything is in accordance with a 'sea lake' – the water colour and size, the numerous bays and an enchanting rocky island right in the middle. A small sea just in front of a spectacular mountain backdrop dominated by the northern Besiberri massif. If you have enough stamina left you should extend the walk by another good half hour to reach the southern tip of the Lac de Mar where meadows and streams offer a delightful spot to stop for a rest.

At the **car park** take the steadily ascending track and follow it as far as the Pontet de Rius. Immediately after the bridge you come to a little house and several signposts where the ascent path starts up to the refuge. On the left of the track and through fir and pine woods the stony path winds its way very steeply uphill – it divides several times and takes some shortcuts. The gradient only relaxes when the large dam wall of Restanca lake comes into view. The path keeps heading straight towards the dam and crosses over to the **Refugi dera Restanca**, 2010m. At the hut you follow the little sign for Llac de Mar and stay at first on the path on the left hand shore. After a stream inlet you first ascend gradually, then more strenuously up the precipitous slope by the lake and reach a level area of meadow. Above the hillside on the left you can see the water streaming out from the underground outlet of the Lac de Mar. Cross over the various branches of the streambed on a little bridge and follow the white and yellow marked path to the other side where it overcomes the incline up an easy zigzag path. After you have climbed up to the threshold of the second valley the path levels out and runs on for a few minutes to the northern tip of **Lac de Mar**, 2235m.

A clear path marked with cairns runs along the left hand side of the lake to the southern end. You reach the southern tip of Lac de Mar over hills and sometimes smaller hillocks, for the most part at some distance from the lake, in order to avoid the numerous bays.

3 Montardo d'Aran, 2833m

Onto the mountain of mountains in the Aran valley

Pònt deth Ressèc – Refugi dera Restanca – Coret d'Oelhacrestada – Montardo d'Aran and back

Location: Artíes, 1140m.
Starting point: car park at the Pònt deth Ressèc, 1395m. (see Walk 2).
Walking times: Pònt deth Ressèc – Refugi dera Restanca 1¾ hrs.; Refugi dera Restanca – Coret d'Oelhacrestada 1½ hrs.; Coret d'Oelhacrestada – Montardo d'Aran 1¼ hrs.; return 4 hrs.; total time 8½ hrs.
Height difference: 1438m.
Grade: technically not a demanding summit ascent, but with a very big variation in height which requires good fitness. You can plan to include an overnight stop at the refuge. GR11-18 as far as the Coret d'Oelhacrestada; very well marked paths with cairns after that to the summit.
Refreshments: Refugi dera Restanca; Artíes.
Tip: there's a 4x4 taxi service from the Pont deth Ressèc to the Pontet de Rius (see page 13.) An alternative route to the Montardo d'Aran starts out from the Refugi Ventosa i Calvell.

Montardo d'Aran is for many a mountain of high symbolic significance. Different to many other remarkable summits, the huge rock pyramid with its steep north face offers an impressive and beautiful picture already as you approach it on the drive through Valartíes, but it also has a splendid view from the surprisingly flat summit. An exciting and scenically first class ascent lies in-between and you should take plenty of time to enjoy it.

Follow the description in Walk 2 as far as the **Refugi dera Restanca**. Continue there along the signposted GR. Ascending the left hand hillside round bends you get gradually closer to the out-flowing stream from the Lac deth Cap deth Pòrt and then go along beside it to reach the regulated lake. Stay on the left hand shore – a tiny neighbouring lake lies hidden nearby behind the chain of hills on the left – and walk along the delightful valley bottom. This turns into a hillside covered in coarse scree at the edge of which you will see a striking pointed rock: the pass you are heading for lies on the right of this. The path stays at first on the left and near to the valley basin, climbs up round a boulder field and then proceeds into the basin full of boulders where GR signs and cairns lead you through the confusion of rocks. Going right, past the pointed rock, you come to the **Coret d'Oelhacrestada**, 2468m, and the boundary of the d'Aigüestortes i Estany de Sant Maurici national park. On the right below the pass lies Estany de Monges, with the Port de Caldes opposite in the east where you cross over to the Refugi de Colomèrs. The path forks beyond the pass: descend on the right if you are going to the Refugi Ventosa i Calvell (see Walk 12), but otherwise stay for a short while on the GR, descend a little and then leave it to the left where there are some obviously placed cairns. Follow a twisting path which climbs up the slope northwards and heads for the broad rock barrier. Even though the path sometimes divides into several parallel ones, it's unlikely that you will get lost due to the numerous cairns. Using these good waymarkers as a guide, you reach the flat southeastern ridge of Montardo. Go to the left here and on the level onto the small col between the jagged pre-summit and the broad crumbly summit ridge.

Views from the summit of Lac deth Cap deth Pòrt, Restanca lake and Lac de Mar.

The path forks at the foot of the mountain: either ascend the eastern slope through broken terrain or on the right hand side of the rocky summit ridge go along the winding well-trodden tracks. It gets very steep again for a short while on either path before finally reaching the summit of **Montardo d'Aran**, 2833m.

4 Refugi de Colomèrs, 2098m, and Lac Obago, 2221m

A taster in the Circ de Colomèrs

Banhs de Tredòs – Refugi de Colomèrs – Lac Obago and back

Location: Salardú, 1280m.
Starting point: car park before the Banhs de Tredòs, 1760m. From Salardú along an asphalt track through the Aiguamòg valley as far as the mandatory car park with information board.
Walking times: Banhs de Tredòs – Refugi de Colomèrs 1¾ hrs.; Refugi de Colomèrs – Lac Obago 1¼ hrs.; return 2½ hrs.; total time 5½ hrs.
Height difference: 490m.
Grade: technically problem-free walk on frequently used paths. Marked in white and yellow as far as the refuge; Gr11 from there onwards.

Refreshments: Ref. de Colomèrs; Salardú.
Tip: there's a 4x4 taxi service from the car park to the hiking path turning off from the track (see page 13).
Alternative: Pòrt de Ratera, 2580m: connecting pass with beautiful views into the eastern national park. Go along the right hand shore of Lac Obago to the southern end where you cross over the inlet stream. Now ascending on the left of the stream and then up the precipitous slope on a zigzag path where the gradient is sustained until just below the flat broad col. Time there and back from Lac Obago 2¼ hrs. Height difference 360m.

Refugi de Colomèrs.

The Circ de Colomèrs is one of the largest and most significant mountain basins in the whole of the Pyrenees. More than 40 lakes are spread through this magnificent granite landscape on different plains and at every turn they provide evidence of the shaping worked by the glaciers from the most recent ice age. This leisurely walk leads past the most beautiful lakes of the region.

As an alternative to the approach along the track take the scenically very beautiful **Camin dera Montanheta**. It starts at the end of the car park on the left hand side of the Arriu d'Aiguamòg, opposite which lie the Banhs de Tredòs (thermal baths with hotel). The path is marked throughout in white and yellow and doesn't present any difficulties. Along the way it touches the track where it is signposted again, crosses the stream later on and then runs on the right of a valley basin through which the stream winds its way: 'Aigüestortes'. (Beautiful viewpoint at the sign for Guardader d'Aigüestortes). Continue through a high valley and then the path meets the track with the sign for 'Colomèrs'. From here proceed along the track or take a shortcut as far as the signpost for the Refugi Colomèrs; after that the track makes a sharp bend and runs out of the valley again. The steep incline now begins on the left through a narrow little valley to an idyllic high plain, the Planhòles dera Lòssa, with meandering streams and the small lake of the same name. Go along the edge of the plain to the sign for 'Ref. Colomèrs' where you turn right and cross over the stream coming from the Colomèrs lake. (The path staying on the right hand side of the stream

also leads to the hut, but with a much steeper incline). The numerous paths on the hillside are proof of how busy the staffed hut is all year round. You come to the left end of the dam wall and walk along it to the **Refugi de Colomèrs**, 2098m.

To continue the walk you need to return to the other end of the dam wall where the GR11 ascends in an easterly direction along a firebreak on the hillside towards a small col between two hills (Coret deth Clòto). Once you reach the col you can see down onto the Lacs de Clòto lying further below. Now it's an easy descent to the long drawn out Lac Long where the path runs along the right hand shore through a wonderful landscape of lakes. Ignore the yellow marked path which turns off right. Adjoining Lac Long is the small Lac Redon which is covered with common water crowfoot at the end of summer. After that, a last comfortable incline brings you to **Lac Obago**, 2221m. A direct continuation of this path goes up the steep north face of Tuc de Ratera with the Pòrt de Ratera on the left below, while Gran Tuc de Colomèrs, the highest peak in this mountain basin, towers up in the south.

5 Long circular walk through the Circ de Colomèrs

Lakes lined up like pearls on a string

Refugi de Colomèrs – Lac deth Port de Colomèrs – Lac de Pòdo – Lac Obago – Refugi de Colomèrs

Location: Salardú, 1280m.
Starting point: Refugi de Colomèrs, 2098m. For access to the hut see Walk 4.
Walking times: total time of the circular walk 4¾ hrs.; an additional 3 hours for the ascent and descent to the refuge.
Height difference: about 600m.
Grade: very demanding walk as regards fitness along the so-called Circuit dels Estanys de Colomèrs. Obvious path with red waymarkings.
Refreshments: Ref. de Colomèrs; Salardú.
Tip: taxi service from the car park as far as the point where the hiking path turns off from the track. The time for the ascent and descent to the refuge is thus shortened by 1¼ hrs. (see page 13).
Alternative: short lake walk in the area of the Lac Major de Colomèrs. The yellow marked path connects the lakes of Garguilhs de Jos, 2200m, and Esthan Plan, 2190m. On the north side of Lac Long it joins with the GR11. Total time there and back from the Refugi de Colomèrs: 1½ hrs.; height difference: 120m.

Seen from above, the mountain valley-shaped basin of Colomèrs looks like a gigantic bowl of rock with countless glistening lakes spreading across the bottom of it. The Circuit dels Estanys de Colomèrs leads past more than a dozen of these 'pearls' and, together with the crossing of the rocky ridge going out from Tuc de Pòdo which actually divides the Circ into two, it also provides you with a view of the whole of this spectacular work of nature.

You begin the circular walk at the **Refugi de Colomèrs** along the white, red and yellow path which ascends the hillside on the right of the reservoir. After only a few minutes the GR turns off right to the Port de Caldes and from here your path is only waymarked in yellow and red. It goes past the old Refugi de Colomèrs and stays for a bit on the sloping shore before overcoming the steep incline of the first hillside. After that you come to **Estanh Mòrt**, 2010m.

Leave the lake on your right hand side and after a short ascent the path forks again: the short walk goes left around the lake and is waymarked in yellow (see Alternative), whereas you continue right and from here the waymarkings consist only of red paint marks. The path heads towards a rock portal which has been cut through by the stream and then gets closer to the stream which you cross where indicated and climb up to the **Lac des Cabidornats**, 2315m.

Lac Obago.

When you reach the lake go left and go past the following small lakes on the right and your path leads up a gentle incline to the **Estanhets deth Pòrt**, 2375m. Numerous lakes lie scattered in the relatively extensive flat terrain of grass and rocks. At the path which then turns off to the Pòrt de Colomèrs keep going straight ahead and you can see ahead the sheer mountain faces at the foot of which lies the **Lac deth Pòrt de Colomèrs**, 2420m. The path then goes past the basin lake on the left and at a distance, then changes its direction and climbs eastwards across rocky slopes and hills.

After a small lake on the right hand side there's an excellent rock shelter lying on the left of the path a little further on. You come to a stream which flows out from a steep valley, turn right onto the hillside, climb up this incline and eventually cross the stream which drains off underneath huge boulders. The best opportunities for looking back across the western half of the Circ are during the ascent. You first reach the **Estanh Gelat**, 2590m, with the conspicuous rocky dome of Tuc de Pòdo towering above, to stand shortly afterwards on the **Còth de Pòdo**, with 2607m, the highest point of the walk.

From the pass you now go steeply downhill to the large **Lac de Pòdo**, 2450m, and reach the shore for a brief moment. The path runs on the right gently ascending past two smaller lakes and then heads towards Lac Obago which is just coming into view and is unmistakable with its scissor-like shape. The now steeply descending path first arrives at **Estanh Solet**, 2270m, and immediately afterwards, at **Lac Obago**, 2221m, it joins with the GR11. Continue to follow this path on the left hand side of the lake, then go past Lac Redon and Lac Long, beyond which the path ascends up to the Coret deth Clòto. From the small col go downhill again to the dam wall and the **Refugi de Colomèrs**.

6 Lacs de Baciver, 2320m

A lovely vista of lakes in the eastern Val d'Aran

Orri – Lac de Baciver – Lacs de Naut de Baciver and back

Location: Baqueira, 1500m.
Starting point: ski lift station Orri, 1860m.
In Baqueira drive in the direction of Plan de Beret; before you reach the large ski coplex take the road sign-posted to the car park of Orri.
Walking times: Orri – Lac de Baciver 1 hr.; Lac de Baciver – Lacs de Naut de Baciver 1 hr.; return 1¾ hrs.; total time 3¾ hrs.
Height difference: 460m.
Grade: easy walk. Waymarkings with cairns.
Refreshments: no refreshments along the way; Baqueira.

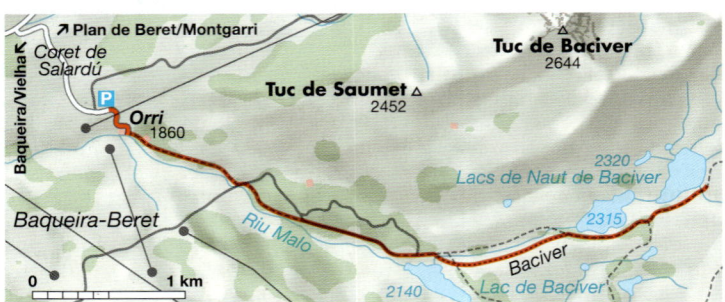

It's hard to imagine that you would find a quiet area of lakes in beautiful mountain surroundings in close proximity to one of the largest ski complexes. You walk through the valley of the Riu Malo to the Lac de Baciver at first and then to the lakes situated higher up which are encompassed by the circle of mountains between Tucs de Baciver, de Marimanha and dera Lança. The open view of the nearby massif of Maladeta with Pico de Aneto is the crowning view of this easy walk.

At the Orri car park go through the access building for the ski lift, past the valley station of the larger lift, then between the restaurant building and the valley station of the small lift directly onto the grass-covered hillside strewn with granite boulders. You will soon see some cairns and the start of an obvious path. After ascending the slope you go through a pretty valley plain on the left of the Riu Malo. Stay on the narrower path on the right at a fork. Between and over granite boulders which have broken off from the rocky ridge on the left above you and now 'plaster' the hillside, head towards the small end of the valley, ascend there a little more steeply and reach the dammed **Lac de Baciver**, 2140m.

Stay at first on the path along the shore on the left of the lake, cross over a little stream and the stream coming from the upper lakes immediately afterwards. Now ascending on the right of the stream across at first pretty, then treeless hillsides, you come to the first of the **Lacs de Naut de Baciver**, 2315m. Continue along the right hand shore until after 10 minutes you have reached the second lake situated just a fraction higher.

On the horizon – Maladeta massif and Pico de Aneto.

7 Tuc de Pèdescauç, 2416m

An inconspicuous peak with a great view

Plan de Beret – Còlh de Clòsos – Tuc de Pèdescauç – Plan de Beret

Location: Baqueira, 1500m.
Starting point: big car park by the ski lift stations of Plan de Beret, 1850m. Accessible from Baqueira along the signposted road.
Walking times: Plan de Beret – Còlh de Clòsos 2¼ hrs.; Còlh de Clòsos – Tuc de Pèdescauç ¾ hr.; Tuc de Pèdescauç – Plan de Beret 1½ hrs.; total time 4½ hrs.
Height difference: about 620m.
Grade: technically straightforward walk which runs for the most part without paths over clear ground. Having a good sense of direction is a distinct advantage at times.
Refreshments: no refreshments along the way; Baqueira.
Alternative: Santuario de Montgarri, 1645m. Place of pilgrimage and much visited chapel near to the deserted hamlet of Montgarri, which was affected by depopulation like many other Pyrenean villages in the 50s and 60s. As described as far as the Cabana de Parros, continue from there along the signposted path which keeps on the left of the Noguera Pallaresa as far as the Santuario. To get to Montgarri, cross over the river on the bridge and then turn to the left. Height difference: 200m. Walking time there and back from the Plan de Beret car park: 2½ hrs.
Tip: the summit point is marked as Cap des Clòsos on different maps and Tuc de Pèdescauç is located to the east of it and mistakenly 50m lower.

Tuc de Pèdescauç is certainly not a mountain in the strict sense of the word, but the enormous view surpasses that of many other mountains. And added to that, you walk through Vall de Parros, a pretty and to a large extent unknown valley which hordes of hikers stream past on their way to the Santuario de Montgarri. Solitude is guaranteed.

At the car park of **Plan de Beret** the big blue building serves as a reference point. Take the forest path which also leads to the Santuario de Montgarri. The track for cars

runs along the other side of the Noguera Pallaresa river on its way to the Santuario. After half an hour you come to Vall de Parros joining from the left and the Cabana de Parros lies on the other side of the valley stream. Leave the Montgarri path which follows the main valley to the right (see Alternative). At the shepherd's hut do not continue along the well-trodden path which turns off northwards, but ascend the right of the stream instead, up the valley.

There are tracks at the start if you're lucky. Then the valley slopes get closer together and you have to climb a little higher to the edge of the forest where there is a relatively clear path. By and large it is maintained as far as the Còlh de Clòsos. After you have avoided the small valley narrowing by going across the wooded slope, the path gets closer to the stream again and runs alongside it. A parallel path runs along the other side of the stream. Gently ascending it continues through the wide valley with softly undulating hillsides which are covered time and again with carpets of bright yellow gen-

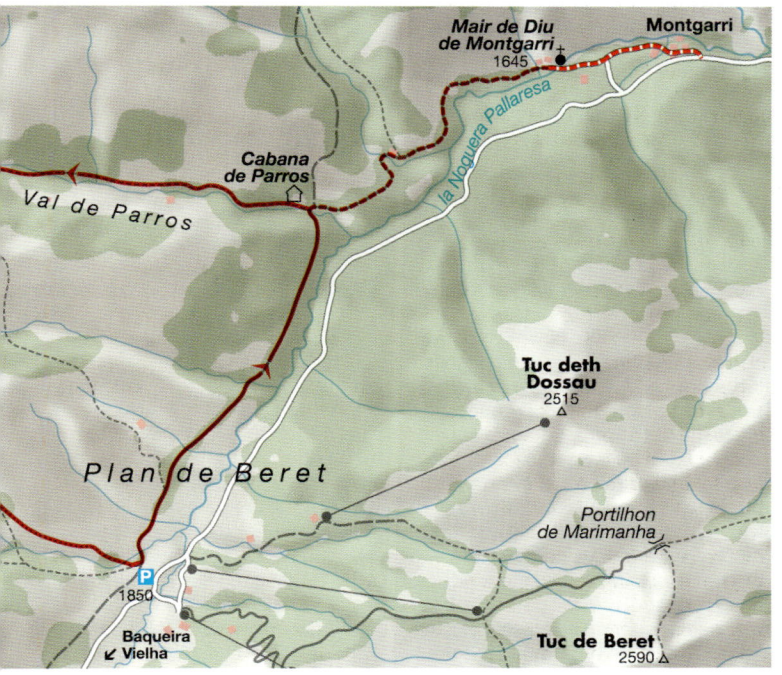

Plan de Beret – in summer an extensive cattle pasture.

tian. After an almost flat section of the path the streambed gets noticeably lower and before that you change over to the other side of the stream and follow the path there (your previous path ascends steeply in the wood to bypass the groove) until the stream bends to the right; it forms a pretty waterfall a bit higher up. A usually dry branch of the stream in summer joins from the left which you now cross over and continue along the path running westwards across the gentle hillsides of the col. You reach the **Còlh de Clòsos**, 2250m, at a small lake. From here on there are no paths. Turn now to the left and head towards the western ridge of Tuc de Pèdescauç across the undulating hills and you will come across several pools in-between. The hillside now becomes stony and steeper but it's an easy climb up to the scarcely defined 'summit' of **Tuc de Pèdescauç**, 2416m.

For the return orientate yourself towards the col between where you are standing and the nearby Tuc de Costarjàs to the south. The two meadow pools on the col are your next intermediary destination. From there follow the path on the left of the pool which runs on the level across the eastern slope of the col. In good time before the valley basin you turn left and head downhill with the lifts and car park already in your sights. The descent across the hillside in places bursting with yellow gentian and heather does not present any problems, you only need to be careful from time to time of small marshy depressions in the area around the rivulets. Keep on the left hand side of the valley which brings you directly back to the **Plan-de-Beret car park**.

View from Tuc de Pèdescauç into the mountains of the national park.

8 Vall de Gerber

Idyllic landscape in a popular side valley

Port de la Bonaigua – Estany de Gerber and back

Location: Baqueira, 1500m.
Starting point: car park on the road above the Port de la Bonaigua, between km 49 and 50, 1900m. Large information board with a map of the hiking routes indicates the car park.
Walking times: car park – Estany de Gerber 1½ hrs.; return 1¼ hrs.; total time 2¾ hrs.
Height difference: 250m.
Grade: problem-free walk on a path waymarked green and orange (Camí de Gerber).
Refreshments: no refreshments along the way; Baqueira.
Linking tip: with Walk 9.

Before the building of the Vielha tunnel the Port de Bon-aigua, more than 2000m high, was the only drivable connection to link the isolated Val d'Aran with the rest of Spain. The pass today is a popular destination for a walk due to its excellent views. It allows you effortless access into the Gerber valley whose quiet charm motivates many visitors in summer to take this short mountain trip.

From the **car park** cross over the road where you will find a signpost for Vall de Gerber. This is the start of your trail which heads into the valley across the hillside. At first go a little downhill to cross over the Riu de la Bonaigua, then gently ascending you walk across the hillside which is at first open, then later covered in pine trees and rhododendron. As you enter the valley the gradient increases and you come to a first lake, the circular Estanyola de Gerber in an idyllic location. Continue along the right of the lake and climb round the step in the valley.

After that the path gets flatter, crosses the valley stream on some rocks and then runs left of a small longish lake to a hillside covered in boulders.

The stream here flows through a broad gap in the rock out of the Gerber lake. On the left of the stream your path starts up the hillside and comes to the **Estany de Gerber**, 2150m, lying in a deep glacial basin.

At the Estanyola de Gerber.

9 Pic d'Amitges, 2851m

Brilliant scenic walk with a summit ascent to finish with

Port de la Bonaigua – Estany de Gerber – Refugi Mataró – Còth der Lac Glaçat – Pic d'Amitges – and back

Location: Baqueira, 1500m.
Starting point: car park on the pass road over the Port de la Bonaigua (see Walk 8).
Walking times: car park – Estany de Gerber 1½ hrs.; Estany de Gerber – Refugi Mataró 1¼ hrs.; Refugi Mataró – Còth der Lac Glaçat ¾ hr.; Coth der Lac Glaçat – Pic d'Amitges 1 hr.; return 3¾ hrs.; total time 8-9 hrs.

Height difference: 951m.
Grade: very long and high grade valley and summit walk demanding special technical skills; waymarked green and orange as far as the Refugi Mataró, then with cairns.
Refreshments: no refreshments along the way; Baqueira.
Tip: the Refugi Mataró is a very well equipped self-catering hut; 16 places.

The normal approach to Pic d'Amitges is made usually from the south, leaving from the Refugi d'Amitges in the d'Aigüestortes i Estany de Sant Maurici national park. The way up through the whole of the Gerber valley takes rather longer, but offers in recompense the combination of a fantastic valley walk with a final ascent to a peak with some of the most beautiful views in the region. It's better to give yourself more time in order to be able to enjoy the diversity of the mountain landscape at leisure.

To the **Estany de Gerber**, 2150m, follow the route described in Walk 8. Immediately after reaching the deep encircled lake the path climbs up left across the hillside round sharp bends to high above the lake. After you have crossed a little side stream continue over boulders where cairns as well as coloured waymarkings guide you along. Then, from the foot of the sheer rocks, climb the steep slope and above that you come to some clearly more level ground. Go past a sign to the Refugi Mataró, and immediately afterwards past a small lake just in front of the Estany Long. The path now runs through a fascinatingly beautiful nature reserve, surrounded by the precipitous mountain rock faces with their sculpted ridges and sharply defined clefts. Ascending slowly again you come to the Estany Redó lying on the left of the path after which there's a really steep section – along the way you are afforded especially beautiful views down the valley and beyond. Then the path levels out again and heads towards the Estany de l'Illa above which on the right the metal **Refugi Mataró**, 2460m, sits majestically on a rocky pedestal.

The path to the hut leads on the right around the granite hill and then climbs uphill for a few metres; the detour is worth it for the view. If you do not want to make a stop here, continue easily between the lake and the rocky eleva-

Destination reached – on Pic d'Amitges.

tion and join the path again on its northern side which comes down from the hut. The path onwards from the hut is now only marked with cairns.
Now descend in a southwesterly direction to the Estany Negre de Dalt which lies at the foot of the Còth der Lac Glaçat. The very obvious pass is your next destination: stay on the left hand side of the lake, cross over the little stream flowing into it and climb through a jumble of large boulders. Cairns reliably guide you along the route which soon becomes more obvious as it changes into a dirt path. In a westerly to southwesterly direction ascend now more steeply, cross a boulder field again and then you reach the right hand hillside of the col where a much clearer path again winds its way up to the **Còth der Lac Glaçat**, 2587m. The lake of the same name lies below the pass and a turn-off from the pass leads to the Refugi de Saborèdo. A tin sign can be found on the pass. From this ascend left further along the

axis of the col up the broad slope going south (be careful here: do not follow the cairns indicating to the right around the ridge leading into a steep valley of scree!), at first over grass and small rocks, in the upper part over boulders and rock slabs. Then the path turns southwestwards and heads along clear tracks – the valley of scree lies on the right below you while precipitous clefts open up on the left – to the col between Tuc de Saborèdo and Pic d'Amitges, the Coll d'Amitges, 2780m.

Just above the col you meet the ascent route to the summit, turn off here to the left and follow the path waymarked with cairns which runs up below the rocky ridge on the western face of the mountain to the **Pic d'Amitges**, 2851m.

A strikingly colourful spot for a base – Refugi Mataró.

Parc Nacional d'Aigüestortes i Estany de St. Maurici

Two valleys running in a west-easterly direction structure the area of today's national park. The valley of the Riu de Sant Nicolau in the west and the valley of Riu Escrita in the east are separated by the Portarró d'Espot. The 2428m high pass was for a long time the traditional crossing for people living in the central valleys who otherwise had to go the long way round the solid line of steep mountains.

Whatever point you set off to in the national park area and its surroundings, you will constantly be aware of the glaciated character of the mountain and valley landscapes for which the national park is famous far and wide. After the Parque Nacional de Ordesa y Monte Perdido, this 'area of 100 lakes' is the most frequently visited region in the Pyrenees. In fact there are about 200 lakes of all sizes in the central and bordering region of the national park, from the high mountain lake at the bottom of the spectacular mountain basin to the wide lake in the valley.

These lakes are impressive evidence of typical glacial landscapes which have their origin in the ice ages of the quaternary period. Due to the movement of the glaciers at that time, the rocky underground was gouged out into hollows and large basins in which the water collected after the melting of the ice masses. When gradually these depressions became filled with erosion material, shallow lakes were formed and eventually sedimented

Taüll is home to famous Romanesque churches.

plains with a covering of plants where the river courses and streams split off many times and the Aigüestortes, literally in Catalan winding waters, were created. With its wonderful meandering streams, meadows of flowers and islands of trees the Planell d'Aigüestortes is a prime example of this geological development. It has also given its name to the western region of the national park. Another phenomenon characterising the landscape is the agglomeration of lakes. Lying mostly in the upper regions they are frequently connected to one another by streams and steep water ledges. This is most evident in the Circ de Colomèrs with at least twelve of the most enchanting mountain lakes and numerous pools – destination of many of the hiking trails.

The dominant types of rock are metamorphic schist, limestone and granite. The dark slate rock occurs especially in the central valleys of San Nicolau, Escrita and Peguera. Compact limestone rock forms, for example, the impressive Encantats at St. Maurici lake which have become the landmark of the national park with their legendary symbolism. The granite is especially striking with its colourfulness and beauty of form, on the one hand in the shape of the smoothly eroded valley floors, round hillocks and striated boulders, on the other in the angular mountain faces and jagged ridges. There's an impressive display of these in the Agulles, literally meaning 'needles', around the Refugis Ventosa i Calvell and Amitges.

Many peaks in the national park waver around the magical 3000m mark. The highest elevation is Pic de Comaloforno with its 3032m, followed by the Besiberri peaks and the Punta Alta de Comalesbienes. If you examine the jagged and steep towering peaks you will generally be under the impression that an ascent of them is only possible for true professionals. But then, on closer inspection, you become aware of the not so difficult approach onto many of the steep massifs and rugged summits from where – for example, Pic d'Amitges, Montardo d'Aran, Tuc de Colomèrs, Tuc de Ratera or Pic de Subenuix – you are afforded fabulous and far-reaching views of the national park. If you confine yourself to the valley or passes, however, your experience of the mountain environment will be no less enjoyable. The big central valleys as well as more inconspicuous side-valleys offer enchanting landscapes and the quiet contemplation of clear mountain streams, flower-covered hillsides, extensive green valleys and lakes in an array of varying tones of colour – and always in the midst of a fascinating mountain backdrop.

There are not any inhabited settlements in the national park. Many of the surrounding villages go back to medieval origin and are home to some well-preserved buildings and structures from that time – defensive towers, castles, churches, monasteries and bridges – Taüll, Boí and Erill-la-Vall at the western entrance to the national park, amongst others, are just as well known for their Romanesque churches as they are for their pretty old village centres.

10 Planell d'Aigüestortes, 1820m

Much visited idyllic landscape in the national park

Entrance to the national park – Estany de Llebreta – Planell d'Aigüestortes and back

Location: Boí, 1250m.
Starting point: car park at the entrance into Vall de Sant Nlcolau, 1380m. At km17 on the L 500 (in the direction of Caldes de Boí) turn right onto a concrete track to the car park. If this is full you will have to park at the La Farga car park on the valley road. A signposted path goes up from there to the starting point.
Walking times: car park – Estany de Llebreta 1½ hrs.; Estany de Llebreta – Planell d'Aigüestortes 1¼ hrs.; return 2½ hrs.; total time 5¼ hrs.
Height difference: 440m.
Grade: technically easy, but long walk on yellow marked path, asphalt in places.
Refreshments: no refreshments along the way; Boí.
Tip: there's a 4x4 taxi service between Boí and Planell d'Aigüestortes (see page 13). Access for bicycles allowed as far as Aigüestortes.
Information is available at the Planell d'Aigüestortes.
Alternative: extension of the walk to the **Aigüestortes de Morrano**, 2160m. This quiet side-valley offers a delightful landscape of streams. From Planell d'Aigüestortes go along the roadway towards Estany Llong, after about 10 minutes turn off right at the sign 'Morrano', go over the bridge and about 200m along the wooden bridge as far as another signpost for Morrano. Continue left here and following the yellow wooden posts, go first through the wood, then across the gradually ascending open slope and past a third signpost. Now without paths go across the sloping meadow up to the sparse stand of pines, diagonally right beside the cairns and onto a relatively well recognisable path. This leads steeply uphill in a southeasterly direction through pines and rhododendron to the flatter exit of the valley. Go left here up the valley above the valley floor with the stream towards the small tree-covered valley. The path keeps to the left hillside at the edge of scree slopes, gently ascending towards the valley, past a conspicuous rock shelter, then descends to the extensive plain of Aigüestortes. Height difference 340m; time there and back from Planell d'Aigüestortes 2¼ hrs.

Aigüestortes, which means 'meandering streams' is an extensive high green plain through which the lovely clear valley stream meanders round islands of trees. It is surrounded by imposing mountains, peaks and jagged rocks, and frequently forms a symbol for the national park. However it does not detract from the other scenic attractions that Vall de Sant Nicolau has to offer on this walk.

The hiking path begins at the **entrance to the national park** on the right of the barrier and is marked with a yellow post. The path you take is the Ruta de la Llúdria, the otter's path. It ascends immediately through a mixed wood on the right hand hillside, then more on the level to the signposted crossing of the Riu de Sant Nicolau. After changing to the other side of the stream the valley then widens out and makes room for sloping meadows while prominent peaks are already coming into view around the Aigüestortes. Here and there thematic information boards have been erected at the side of the path. Now paved in natural stone the path runs a little way from the stream, goes up a gentle incline, crosses the access road, passes a hut, briefly touches the access road and then runs across the cleared hillside to huts and the Ermita de Sant Nicolau. According to the information board the pilgrimage church is dedicated to the protection from storms, snow and hail. Legend has it that the crowns of French kings are buried nearby. Those who find them will drop dead on the spot. Every year on the first Sunday in July the inhabitants of Boí go on a pilgrimage.

Aigüestortes.

Now go down the old roadway to the **Estany de Llebreta**, 1620m. Go a short way along the track, then immediately turn off right and through the valley bottom beside the stream. The path heads for the beautifully formed waterfalls, climbs the slope and half way up you come to a *mirador* with a really close-up view of the Cascada de Sant Esperit. As you continue the walk you briefly touch the access road again twice, then you join an old roadway along which you reach a lovely grassy plateau with granite boulders. A signpost points left here, but you stay just above the valley bottom and meet the track from which you go left after a few metres, then cross it and arrive at the Font de Sant Esperit. After the spring go again to the concrete track which brings you in a few minutes to the place where you wait for taxis and a few steps further on, to the **Planell d'Aigüestortes**, 1820m.

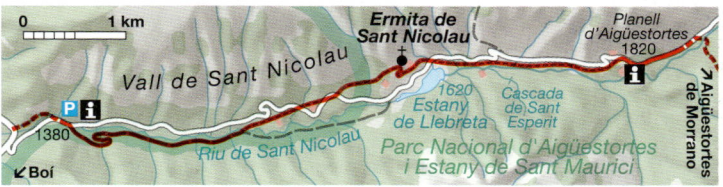

11 Portarró d'Espot, 2424m

To the classic pass in the national park

Planell d'Aigüestortes – Estany Llong – Portarró d'Espot – Mirador de St. Maurici and back

Location: Boí, 1250m.
Starting point: Planell d'Aigüestortes, 1820m (see Walk 10).
Walking times: Planell d'Aigüestortes – Estany Llong 1¼ hrs.; Estany Llong – Portarró d'Espot 1½ hrs.; Portarró d'Espot – Mirador de St. Maurici ¼ hr.; return 2½ hrs.; total time 5½ hrs.
Height difference: 604m.
Grade: long walk without any technical demands; roadway and frequently used hiking path.
Refreshments: Ref. d'Estany Llong; Boí.
Alternative: Pic del Portarró, 2728m. Good summit, which rises to the north of Portarró, for views across the surrounding mountains. The path sets off on the right of the broad mountain base, winds uphill and then swings onto the broken ridge. With a tendency to go left, it ascends up to the rocky summit. Walking time there and back from Portarró d'Espot: 1½ hrs.

The walk from the Planell d'Aigüestortes to Portarró d'Espot gives you an excellent impression of the mountain landscape in the western central valley of the national park. Since the view from the pass into the St.-Maurici valley is restricted, it is worth making the short detour to the *mirador* – an ideal viewpoint where you can stop for a rest. Many hikers are content to walk just along the easy section as far as the pretty location of Estany Llong which is the best stopping-off point.

At the **Planell d'Aigüestortes** follow the roadway along the Riu de Sant Nicolau. It keeps on the left of the stream to the wide valley pastures, the Prats d'Aiguadassi, in which streams from various directions all join to-

At Estany Llong.

gether. Go across wooden bridges over the valley plain which is running with streams and follow the roadway on the other side which ascends through the wood and goes past the Refugi d'Estany Llong. A little later the **Estany Llong**, 2000m, comes into view, while further in the east lies Portarró d'Espot rising up to the left of Pic del Portarró. Along beside the lake you come to the grassy Planell d'Estany Llong which serves as pastureland in summer. Immediately after a wooden bridge over a side stream the path divides: left goes to the Estany Redó, but you keep straight ahead along the broad bridle path and then you have the chance of making a detour to a kind of tree memorial: the signposted 'Pi de Peixerani' is an old pine tree of stately dimensions (it takes 10 minutes along the grassy path turning off to the right). Then the path ascends steeply and goes round leisurely bends on which you continue to gain height and enjoy increasingly better views. Look back on the left to the Estany Llong and now too on the Estany Redó surrounded by precipitous slopes with cascading waterfalls. Impressive mountain chains rise up in the northwest around Gran Tuc de Colomèrs and in the southeast, the jagged rock bastions around Pic de Subenuix. The broad Portarró d'Espot comes into view and the path heads at first towards it on the right hand side, then swings left over to the slopes of Pic del Portarró and runs across them up to **Portarró d'Espot**, 2424m, where there's a tiny lake. At the pass follow the signs for the Mirador de St. Maurici. The path marked with a yellow wooden post goes off to the south, quickly changes direction to the south east and runs along the foot of the debris strewn Agulla del Portarró to the most beautifully situated *mirador* with an extensive view into the Maurici valley and the dramatic peaks of the Amitges region.

12 Refugi Ventosa i Calvell, 2242m

The Besiberri massif is a dominant presence throughout

Estany de Cavallers – Refugi Ventosa i Calvell and back

Location: Boí, 1250m.
Starting point: Estany de Cavallers, 1780m. Take the valley road to Caldes de Boí, continue along the asphalt track to the car park at the reservoir. If this is full you will need to park in one of the car parks lower down.

Walking times: Estany de Cavallers – Refugi Ventosa i Calvell 2¼ hrs.; return 2 hrs.; total time 4¼ hrs.
Height difference: 462m.
Grade: no problems on this half day walk along yellow waymarked hiking paths.
Refreshments: Ref. Ventosa i Calvell; Boí.

The ascent to the Refugi Ventosa i Calvell is a classic hut walk. From here you can walk over the pass to the Refugis dera Restanca and de Colomèrs. Not only is the ever present Besiberri massif with the two 3000m peaks a feast for the eyes, so too is the actual valley and mountain landscape through which this walk leads.

From the car park go to the **Estany de Cavallers** reservoir where the waymarked hiking path starts. Changing from a gentle up-and-down it runs across the slope of the shoreline to the north end of the lake where it then begins to ascend some bends. The scenery is characterised by the soft, smooth and at times striated granite hummocks, a typical feature of glacial activity. After the ascent you come to a long drawn out high plain, the meadows of which are scored with side streams. The Planell de Riumalo is a strategic point for the ascent to the northern Besiberri peak and in summer there will usually be a lot of tents here. At the bridge over the stream keep going straight ahead and walk through the Planell to the bridge over the outlet of the Estany Negre. Cross over it, enter the national park (sign) and climb the valley ledge keeping on the right of the Barranc de les Llastres. On the left of the path directly at the start you see a rock which is almost completely cut through by this mountain stream. Continue up a moderate incline and the path goes round a steep rocky knoll, away from the stream and through a narrow gap

Besiberri massif – the most famous 3000er in the national park.

in the rock. Keep ascending until you reach a section of the valley with a captivating landscape of rocky outcrops, green pastures, rivulets, knotty pines and pretty waterfalls and ledges. In-between times there are cairns to guide you across smooth rock and then the path runs once more through a pretty valley until eventually the Estany Negre and the huts above the eastern end of the lake come into view. The path stays above the lake, then sets off in a northeasterly direction uphill and after crossing the stream runs over to the **Refugi Ventosa i Calvell**, 2242m.

13 Vall Fosca and its lakes

Conflicting impressions of the civilised mountain world

Embassada de Sallente – Estany Gento – Refugi de Colomina – Estany de Saburó and back

Location: Cabdella, 1420m.
Starting point: car park at the right hand end of the Embassada de Sallente, 1770m. From Senterada go along the road through Vall Fosca as far as the reservoir.
Walking times: Embassada de Sallente – Estany Gento 1¼ hrs.; Estany Gento – Refugi de Colomina 1 hr.; Refugi de Colomina – Estany de Saburó 1 hr.; return 3 hrs.; total time 6¼ hrs.
Height difference: 755m.
Grade: long walk on marked paths, GR 11-20 from Estany Gento.
Refreshments: bar-restaurant at Estany Gento; Refugi de Colomina.
Tip: a cable railway runs from the Sallente reservoir to the Estany Gento between July and September (at the north end of the lake, where there's a car park too), although the timetable is rather restricted. In summer 2003 the times were: daily; depart 9.00 and 15.00, return 13.00 and 18.00. ✆ 973.663001 and 973.252231.
Alternative: return along the eastern side of the lakes. At the eastern end of the Estany de Saburó reservoir a grassy path goes off to the south marked with cairns. Gently descending it keeps on the left of a *barranco* dropping sharply down to the Estany de Mar and meets a cross path which you follow to the left. This path quickly descends to the Estany de Mar and then runs a little away from and out of sight of the lake through a pretty countryside of grassy hillsides, rocks and brooks. Following cairns you go round a side stream, cross over the furrow of a stream and arrive at the reservoir. Continue on the left of it, then along a path on the north side of the Estany Frescau. At the end of the lake there's a short crossing over a small col beyond which the Estany de Colomina comes into view. The path runs downhill and eventually levels out as it runs over to the refuge. Another ½ hr. approximately.

The view of the Estany Gento is not exactly breathtaking since the installations for electricity production are all too prevalent. However, further up, the mountain surroundings have still managed to preserve their wildness together with an idyllic tranquility – small relics like the old lorry track right through the middle of the rocky wastes are more amusing than disturbing. Pic de Peguera, which is only just a few metres short of the 3000m mark, is undoubtedly the eye-catcher in these rugged mountain ranges.

At the car park at the **Embassada de Sallente** your path is signposted Ref. Colomina. It goes off right and ascends easy bends up the eastern hillside above the reservoir. A few bends past the wooden posts you have the alternative of either continuing up directly through the valley along well-trodden paths or going right along the more leisurely hillside path which first goes up round some bends and then crosses the slope to finally meet the shortcut again. A rail track runs across the path at a signpost near to a spring. Continue left here in accordance with the sign for Estany Gento. The path levels out high above the reservoir. You pass four tunnels along the way and after the last one, the **Estany Gento**, 2140m, comes into view.

Pic de Peguera.

Walk over to the cable car where the hiking path continues as a GR trail. Well-constructed, it runs across hillsides covered with boulders (ignore a GR turn-off to the left), then zigzags uphill where the gradient gets less again and at a new rail track you come to a fork. The southern tip of Estany Tort lies over to the left and you turn right, go a little way along the rails and turn left at a rocky path. It winds across slopes strewn with large chunks of rock to a ruin near to the Estany de Colomina where the path goes off right to the **Refugi de Colomina**, 2395m.

Following the sign for the Coll de Peguera / Coll de Saburó left, continue your walk on the left hand shore of the lake – the steep slopes are scattered with gigantic boulders broken off from the Pales de Colomina – and at a small dam reach the Estany de Mar lying only a few metres higher up. Continue along the level path on the left of the lake, the colour of which near to the shore appears to turn azure blue at times, and head towards the Pas de l'Ós. The steep pass enables you to cross the northern slopes of Estany de Mar and is immediately recognisable by the huge rock table and a projecting tower between which the path reaches the pass. At first paved with rock, it then turns into a dirt path and further up leads steeply uphill in steps. After the Pas de l'Ós head towards the dam until you reach the **Estany de Saburó**, 2525m.

14 Walk around the Estany de St. Maurici, 1915m

In the company of the mountains of the national park

Prat de Pierró – Estany de St. Maurici – Refugi E. Mallafré – Prat de Pierró

Location: Espot, 1310m.
Starting point: Prat de Pierró, 1650m. The car park with an information board is reached along a signposted road from Espot before the national park boundary.
Walking times: Prat de Pierró – Estany de St. Maurici 1¼ hrs.; Estany de St. Maurici – Refugi Mallafré 1hr; Refugi Mallafré – Prat de Pierró 1 hr.; total time 3¼ hrs.
Height difference: 265m.
Grade: easy circular walk on marked paths throughout. Section on the GR11.
Refreshments: Refugi E. Mallafré; Espot.
Tip: 4x4 taxi will take you there and collect you later (see page 13).

The Encantats covered in snow in May.

The walk to and round the Estany de St. Maurici gives you a first impression of the natural beauty of the national park without any great exertion. The Encantats, sheer twin peaks with mystical significance, are like a landmark on the way through the mountain scenery. According to legend, two hunters of chamois were turned to stone in the form of sharp pointed crags in the cleft between them because they made fun of the pilgrims on their way from St. Maurici to the chapel.

At the end of the car park on the **Prat de Pierró** turn off right from the road (sign for Estany). Walk along a wooden walkway as far as the bridge over the Riu Escrita and join the GR on the other side of the stream. Keeping on the right of the stream the broad path runs through the charming valley countryside, crosses the track on its way and gets closer to the stream. After a section where you rapidly gain height and briefly come into contact with the track the path becomes flatter. The Encantets become more and more impressive. The path widens out considerably, leads across a wooden bridge and afterwards goes past the St.Maurici chapel on the right hand side and reaches a fork a little later which is the point of your return path from around the lake: a sign on the left indicates the Refugio Mallafré, but you keep going in the direction of **Estany de St. Maurici**, 1915m, where there's a little information board on the right.

Now walk along the white and yellow marked path signposted to Volta l'Estany / Cascada. In a gentle up-and-down it keeps to the shoreline lined chiefly with birch trees as far as the fork where the path up to the Cascada continues right. However, stay on the Volta l'Estany route now going through hefty pine trees and down to the level of the lake, cross a stream on a little wooden bridge and follow the narrow shore path to the western tip of the lake. A wooden bridge leads over the incoming Barranco del Portarró and a little later you balance across tree trunks over the Barranco de Subenuix The path then runs across wooded slopes on the southern side of the lake. Almost immediately again at the other end of the lake, concrete steps help you over a small protrusion and after that you turn off right from the lake following the signpost for Refugi Mallafré and about 50m before some signposts go left along the roadway down to the **Refugi E. Mallafré**, 1885m. From there follow the roadway (sign for Estany / Aparcament) and meet the valley path again at the fork.

15 Estany Negre de Peguera, 2330m

Through Vall de Peguera to the deepest lake in the national park

Pont de Feners – Estany de Lladres – Estany Negre and back

Location: Espot, 1310m.
Starting point: Pont de Feners, 1320m, in Espot. From Espot drive in the direction of Superespot where you can park on the track turning off right before the bridge. Look out for the sign for Estany Negre.
Walking times: Pont de Feners – Estany de Lladres 2 hrs.; Estany de Lladres – Estany Negre 1¼ hrs.; return 3 hrs.; total time 6¼ hrs.
Height difference: 1010m.
Grade: long walk with a big variation in height; GR 11-20.
Refreshments: Refugi J.M.Blanc at Estany Tort de Peguera; Espot.
Tip: there's a 4x4 taxi service to take you there and collect you later (see page 13).

The varied scenery of the Peguera valley with its sheer mountain backdrop around Estany Negre is revealed on this demanding walk up to the extensive lakes in the eastern part of the national park unfolds. The 'black lake' is is the largest of the more than a dozen lakes which can be discovered in this area on a hike lasting several hours. However, you would need to spend the night in the nearby Refugi J.M.Blanc which is also the base for the ascent up to Pic de Peguera and the crossing of the Saburó pass to the lakes in Vall Fosca.

Distant view into the Pyrenean border mountains.

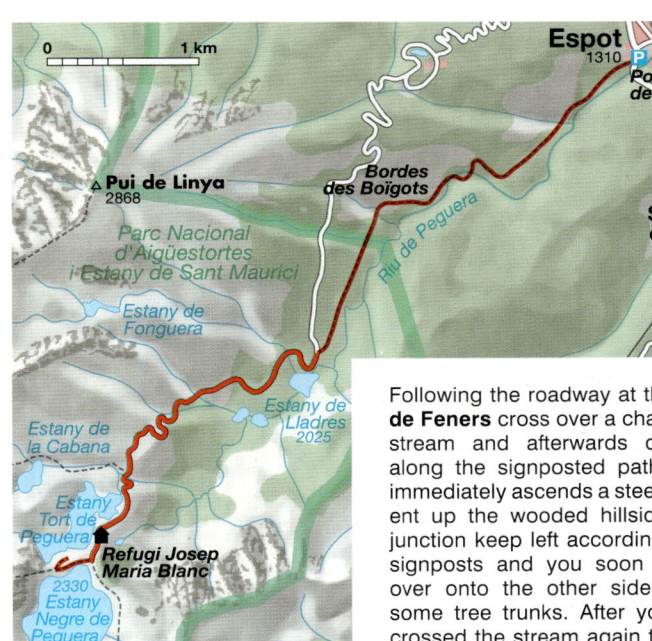

Following the roadway at the **Pont de Feners** cross over a channelled stream and afterwards continue along the signposted path which immediately ascends a steep gradient up the wooded hillside. At a junction keep left according to the signposts and you soon change over onto the other side across some tree trunks. After you have crossed the stream again the path leads onto an open slope with the sparse remains of Bordes des Boïgots. The view down the valley gives you a tiny foretaste of the superb panoramic views which await you at the top. The steep gradient of the path eases up a little. You enter the national park and walk through the grassy, granite strewn hillsides of Planell de la Trapa. A wooden bridge runs through marshy land and takes you to the dammed lake called **Lladres**, 2025m. Take the old roadway leading away from the lake and straight away you will reach the approach track. It goes up round bends to the beautifully formed mountain basin and leads past Estany Tort de Peguera where the Refugi J.M.Blanc is situated. A path turns off right to the hut, but you continue along the roadway to reach after a few minutes the **Estany Negre de Peguera**, 2330m. The dark blue lake is dominated by the jagged ridge between the Pics de Sudorn and de la Mainera. A place to stop for a rest with scenic views is quickly reached if you follow the signposts to the right and the GR waymarkers at the dam wall and climb the small hill by the shore.

16 Through the Vall de Monestero

An excursion through a charming valley

St. Maurici – Estany de Monestero and back

Location: Espot, 1310m.
Starting point: St. Maurici, 1915m. For approach on foot or by car see Walk 14.
Walking times: St. Maurici – Estany de Monestero 1½ hrs.; return 1¼ hrs.; total time 2¾ hrs.
Height difference: 290m.
Grade: easy valley walk.

Refreshments: Refugi E. Mallafré; Espot.
Tip: 4x4 taxi will take you as far as St. Maurici and collect you later (see page 13).
Linking tip: with Walk 17: Pic de Monestero. The walk as far as the wonderful head of the valley is also very rewarding without the summit ascent.

Hillside of flowers, light pine woods, grassy plains, lakes, a pretty stream and last but not least a large backdrop with Pic de Peguera in the middle – Vall de Monestero to the south of the St.-Maurici lake provides you with everything for a pleasant walk.

In **St. Maurici** a roadway turns off left from the asphalt approach road which is the hiking path coming up from Espot. Walk a few minutes down this path as far as a roadway branching off to the right which you follow to the Refugi E. Mallafré and a little further to the signposted junction. The walk into the Monestero valley begins to the left here. Climb quickly up the right hand side of the valley stream and after a while the path flattens out and leads through luxuriant meadows of flowers and thin pine trees while some striking peaks come into view at the end of the valley. Cross a depression in the valley with meandering streams and small islands of trees. A lengthy wooden plank takes you to the other side of the valley and after an easy incline you change over to the other side again.

The path now ascends more steeply up the right hand hillside and reaches the Prat de Monestero. Cross the pretty pastureland, ascend leisurely up through small thin pine woods and you then come to a valley full of debris. Climb up through the boulder-strewn hillside, where the path levels out again and continue for a short way over some boulders before coming to the **Estany de Monestero**, 2175m.

In the upper Monestero valley.

17 Pic de Monestero, 2878m

Onto the small neighbour of Pic de Peguera

St. Maurici – Estany de Monestero – Coll de Monestero – Pic de Monestero and back

Location: Espot, 1310m.
Starting point: St. Maurici, 1915m. For access on foot or by car see Walk 14.
Walking times: St. Maurici – Estany de Monestero 1½ hr.; Estany de Monestero – Coll de Monestero 2 hrs.; Coll de Monestero ½ hr.; return 3 hrs.; total time 7 hrs.
Height difference: 993m.
Grade: long and demanding summit ascent with many steep sections; airy summit region. Path waymarked with paint or cairns.
Refreshments: Refugi E. Mallafré; Espot.
Tip: 4x4 taxi will take you as far as St. Maurici and collect you later (see page 13).

When you reach the Coll de Monestero your gaze will at first fall on Pic de Peguera naturally enough which, according to the map, falls 17 metres short of the 3000m mark. Pic de Monestero lying opposite, a good 100m lower, might stand in its shadow, but the panoramic views are just as good from here as from its higher neighbour.

From **St. Maurici** to **Estany de Monestero** follow the route in Walk 16. Continue along the right hand shore through dense yarrow to a valley meadow with yellow post waymarkers. The path forks just before some logs take you across the stream: a path goes left along beside the waymarkers and keeps to the left hand side of the valley and ascends above the basin at the head of the valley where you have to rely on the cairns to find your way through sections of hillside strewn with boulders. This path meets the grassy path again which turns off right further up and which you follow as it runs through the pretty head of the valley. It first crosses side streams, then keeps close to the valley stream on the right before changing onto the left hand side across some stepping stones just before a conspicuous hill covered in pines. Continue between hillside and stream up to the end of the valley where the path steers southwards towards the enormous Tossal del Mig with a rock dome, but then turns to the left and ascends very steeply up the eastern hillside of the head of the valley. It joins with the yellow waymarked path and then there's a fork at which you follow the signpost left to the Coll de Monestero (straight on brings you to the Coll de Peguera). Now go uphill across less steep slopes covered in grass and rhododendrons, past a rock shelter and afterwards you come to the edge of a deep hollow, the bottom of which is covered with huge boulders. Keeping at about the same height the path runs on the right above the hollow and then turns into the valley with the steep Monestero pass which veers up left to Pic de Monestero. Stay at first on the now boulder-strewn hillside at the foot of Pic de Peguera, then the path swings onto the slope of the pass where several tracks wind clearly uphill directly to the top. The ascent of the steep slope over fine scree can be rather tiresome and, if necessary, keep further left on the coarser scree and solid rock.

Go left along the **Coll de Monestero**, 2715m, and along the path parallel to the crest of the col. The path heads towards the southwest ridge of the peak, ascends a bit and then runs on the right of the heavily boulder-strewn ridge. In the upper third section the path turns diagonally right onto the mountain ridge and crosses over to the long rocky eastern ridge. Go left there to **Pic de Monestero**, 2878m.

Summit destination of Pic de Monestero.

18 Vall and Pic de Subenuix, 2949m

Onto one of the most attractive summits in the national park

St. Maurici – Estany de Subenuix – Pic de Subenuix and back

Location: Espot, 1310m.
Starting point: St. Maurici, 1915m. For access on foot or by car see Walk 14.
Walking times: St. Maurici – Estany de Subenuix 1¼ hrs.; Estany de Subenuix – Pic de Subenuix 2¼ hrs.; return 3 hrs.; total time 6½ hrs.
Height difference: 1064m.
Grade: demanding summit walk over sometimes difficult terrain (extensive boulder field and very steep ascent up to the pass) with waymarker cairns; a bit of climbing (maximum Grade I) in the summit area. Experience needed in climbing over boulders. Yellow waymarkings as far as Estany de Subenuix.
Refreshments: Refugi E. Mallafré; Espot.
Tip: 4x4 taxi will take you as far as St. Maurici and collect you later (see page 13).

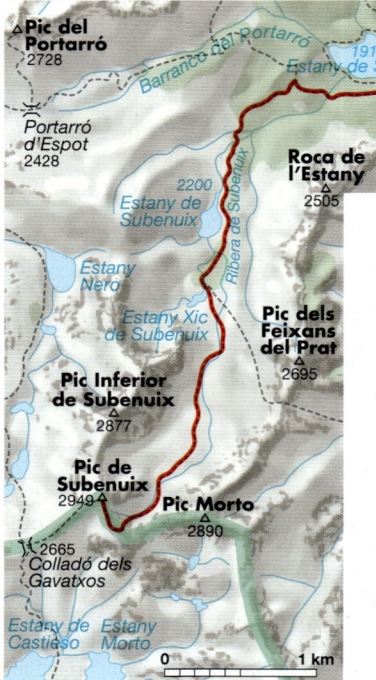

In spite of its wonderfully attractive scenery Vall de Subenuix is much less frequented in comparison to the other valleys. Perhaps this is because it is relatively short and there are enormous boulder fields beyond the delightful small lake which give you the impression that the valley is blocked and impassable. You will be rewarded on this walk with wonderful scenic contrasts and the unbroken view from the summit of Subenuix is truly spectacular.

In **St. Maurici**, just before the information board, a roadway turns off left from the tarmac road. This is the hiking path that comes up from Espot which you descend for a few minutes until you reach a roadway

Pic de Subenuix: summit view to the south.

branching off right. Follow this to the Refugi Ernest Mallafré and a bit further on to the junction: Subenuix is signposted to the right.

Go along the broad forest path which starts here above the St.-Maurici lake to the signposted junction shortly after you have crossed the Barranc de Subenuix on a wooden bridge. Turn left from the path which continues to the Portarró d'Espot. Marked with yellow wooden posts it leads across green slopes and through groups of light pine trees and rhododendron. After a short steeper incline you reach a valley plain. Walk across the plain along a level path to the **Estany de Subenuix**, 2200m, situated in front of an imposing backdrop of crags. The clearly identifiable path keeps on the left above the lake and is waymarked with cairns. Further beyond it moves closer to the lake which you cross over on the stepping stones and ascends the valley up a moderate incline to the Estany Xic de Subenuix where there's a rocky island in the middle. Directly past the lake on the left begins a chaotic area covered in broken rocks of all sizes. Well positioned cairns guide you across and over the boulders.

The path goes over the following hill, covered with rhododendron and broken rock, on the left hand side and avoids the rocks. The steep ascent – with a scree slope lying below on the left – brings you to the top of the hill where you find yourself standing in front of a large area strewn with rock debris. Cross over this keeping in a south-southwesterly direction towards a broad hillside streaked with grassy areas where you can clearly see signs of a path. The ground becomes grassier again with the odd boulder lying about. Then there's another slope covered in broken rock – a steep incline to the southwest helps you to negotiate it – and a wide scree slope spreads out ahead. From here in a south-southwest direction you can see the left hand half of the pass going up to Pic Mòrto Dann. The col extends on the left where the ridge rises with a gentle incline to a pointed tower. The jagged crest on the right is in reality only a ridge of rock that divides the col. Your destination of the right hand half of the pass still cannot be seen. In front of you the path now heads towards a broad and very steep scree slope. At first it stays on the right of the valley basin strewn with large rocks, then it runs quite a distance over to the middle to avoid the steep cones of debris at the foot of the right hand side of the hillside.

Now you can see further ahead: in the middle of the slope to the col there are well-trodden tracks across the scree which lead up directly to the now visible pass. They form an unpleasantly shifting path which makes the ascent (in comparison to the descent!) extremely arduous. It's advisable to cross over right beforehand to the foot of the rocky slopes and then climb up beside these. Good compacted scree and handholds and footholds in the rock make the ascent to the pass significantly easier. But you then have to cross back over towards the col in good time otherwise you will find yourself having to do some proper climbing. On the pass turn right and follow the problem-free ridge and go round a small hump of rock on the left hand side. After that there's a bit of scrambling and you are soon standing on the narrow **Pic de Subenuix**, 2949m.

Pic Inferior de Subeniuix, your destination's smaller 'brother'.

19 Pòrt de Ratera, 2580m, and Tuc de Ratera, 2862m

A much walked pass with the most superb views

St. Maurici – Pòrt de Ratera – Tuc de Ratera and back

Location: Espot, 1310m.
Starting point: St. Maurici, 1915m. For access on foot or by car see Walk 14.
Walking times: St. Maurici – Pòrt de Ratera 2½ hrs.; Pòrt de Ratera – Tuc de Ratera ¾ hr.; return 2¾ hrs.; total time about 6 hrs.
Height difference: 947m.
Grade: unproblematic walk at first along yellow marked path, then along the GR as far as the Pòrt de Ratera; really steep incline up to Tuc de Ratera on well-trodden path, amply marked with cairns; a tiny bit of scrambling up to the summit.
Refreshments: no refreshments along the way; Espot.
Tip: 4x4 taxi will take you as far as St. Maurici and the Refugi d'Amitges and col-

View from Tuc de Ratera.

lect you later (see page 13).
Alternative: return via the Refugi d'Amitges, 2380m. Scenically beautiful end to the walk with imposing mountain backdrop of, amongst others, the two towers of the Agulles d'Amitges. From the pass take the alternative path running above on the left (marked with yellow posts) to the signpost for the Refugi d'Amitges. Turn left here and the path runs across the slopes of the Sierra de Saborèdo, crosses a lengthy boulder slope guided by cairns, then it forks. Continue left and climb steeply up onto the ridge of the valley divide between Ratera and Amitges valley. The prettily situated lakes come unexpectedly into view, the path descends suddenly and runs along the long-drawn-out chain of hills between the two lakes over to the track. Go right there to the nearby Refugi d'Amitges and along the approach road down to the Estany de Ratera. Time for the return to this point: 1¼ hrs.

The ascent through the long valley to the Pòrt de Ratera provides you with varying landscapes at every turn and delightful views of unspoiled nature. It's not without good reason that the GR11 runs over this pass which connects St. Maurici with the idyllic lakes in the Circ de Colomèrs. The ascent of Tuc de Ratera is no longer part of the long distance path, but if possible, you should plan this into your walk – the view is breathtaking and one of the best that the mountains of the national park has to offer.
Begin the walk in **St. Maurici** along the lakeside path running on the right of the Estany de St. Maurici as far as the junction where the walk round the lake starts (Volta l'Estany). Take the path on the right to the Cascada and

ascend a shady wood to the spectacular waterfall where you come to the signpost for Estany de Ratera. The path continues to ascend and moves away from the mountain stream and comes to a second similar signpost. Set off up the steep forest path on the left and you meet the track and the GR which followed it from St. Maurici. This is the approach track to the Refugi d'Amitges. Follow it to the left, cross over the Riu de Ràtera and proceed into the pretty valley of the Estany de Ratera. Once past the lake you leave the track to the left at the signpost for Pòrt de Ratera and the roadway at the edge of a small depression in the valley brings you quickly to another signpost where you take the right hand hiking path through the most beautiful landscape of streams. After you have crossed the stream on some logs the Estany de les Obagues de Ratera soon comes into view. At the junction where it goes right to the Refugi d'Amitges (waymarked yellow), keep going straight ahead and the path descends briefly to the lake and then immediately ascends again up the hillside. You can see the pass in the foreground, dominated by Tuc de Ratera on the left. As you walk up the valley, gradually ascending more steeply again, the path keeps changing sides in the valley to avoid slopes strewn with boulders. Already close to the pass it then ascends an incline which forms a kind of valley dividing line. The steep slope brings you above the Estany del Cap del Pòrt de Ratera lying at the foot of the pass. Further ahead the path then forks to join up again briefly before the pass: the left path steeply ascends the hillside of the col while the right hand path runs round a longish, but more gently inclined bend. At the sign for the Parque Nacional you enter the wide **Pòrt de Ratera**, 2580m, where a small lake lies hidden a few steps further to the right The edge of this lake is often iced over at the edge well into late summer. The wide and hilly countryside of the pass consisting of grass and rocks make this an excellent place to stop for a rest and enjoy the views.

The ascent to Tuc de Ratera starts at the national park sign. A path marked throughout with cairns leaves the pass here to the south and immediately begins to ascend. After a while it bends to the southwest and then swings onto the sheer southern face of the mountain to make a direct approach up to the summit. Following the narrow and at times steep bends, there's a lengthy section of zigzags which lead to a tiny col which drops away abruptly to the north side. Go up to the left here (on the right lies an only slightly lower pre-summit). A bit of clambering up some rocks and you are standing on the top of **Tuc de Ratera**, 2862m, where you can enjoy almost never ending panoramic views.

Stunningly beautiful places to stop as you make your way up to the summit.

20 Refugi d'Amitges, 2380m

Into a bizarre area of crags by a circuitous route

St. Maurici – Mirador de l'Estany – Refugi d'Amitges and back

Location: Espot, 1310m.
Starting point: St. Maurici, 1915m. For access see Walk 14.
Walking times: St. Maurici – Mirador de l'Estany 1½ hrs.; Mirador de l'Estany – Refugi d'Amitges 1¼ hrs.; return 2¼ hrs.; total time 5 hrs.
Height difference: 495m.

Grade: long walk posing no problems along marked paths.
Refreshments: Refugi d'Amitges; Espot.
Alternative: return either along the approach track or via the Cascada de Ratera (For access see Walk 19).
Linking tip: with Walk 19.

Just like a bizarre rock cathedral the Agulles d'Amitges are the undisputed point of attention in a mountain region which has even more to offer in the way of fantastic rock formations and jagged peaks. Right in the middle lies the famous and comfortable hut to which you can take some delightful detours instead of walking along the track.

In **St. Maurici** a roadway turns off left from the asphalt approach road before the information board. This is the hiking path coming up from Espot. Descend this path for a few minutes to a roadway which branches off to the right and which brings you to the Refugi Ernest Mallafré and a bit further on to a junction. Go right here in the direction of Portarró along the broad forest path via St. Maurici lake.

Cross the Barranc de Subenuix on a wooden plank and ignore the following turn-off left into the Subenuix valley. At first continue up a moderate incline and then more steeply uphill to reach a signposted fork where you leave the path going to the Portarró d'Espot.

Continue right towards the *mirador*, immediately cross the Barranc del Portarró, and then follows a lengthy and extensively flat section across a hillside with another stream crossing. At first descending, then ascending again, you come to a cross path. Along this path to the left brings you to the **Mirador de l'Estany**, 2170m. The viewing platform with a board indicating what can be seen from this point offers a privileged view of the St. Maurici mountains. Go back and continue along the hiking path which be-

Like a rock cathedral – the pointed spires of the Agulles d'Amitges.

comes a roadway further on. At the point where the GR turns off to the Pòrt de Ratera, leave the roadway and ascend the valley for a little way.
The valley stream is crossed and you now stay on the right hand side as far as the sign for the Refugi d'Amitges where you turn off right along the path marked with yellow wooden posts. The path goes over the hill-shaped valley divide and joins the access track to the hut. Continue left here and immediately past a contained spring there are a few steep bends to negotiate before you arrive at the **Refugi d'Amitges**, 2380m.

21 Estany de la Gola, 2249m

Another hot tip – Valle de Unarre

Cerbi – Estany de la Gola and back

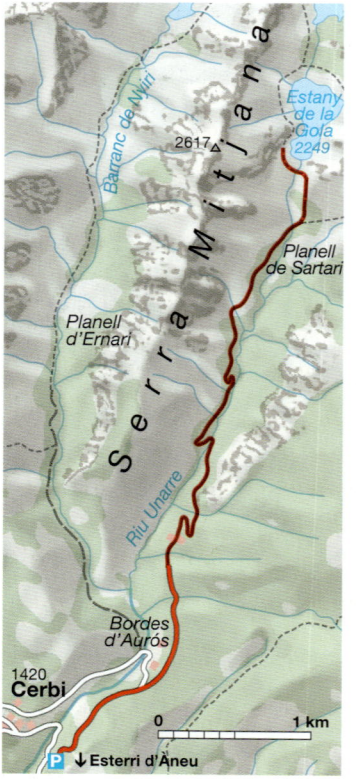

Location: Esterri d'Àneu, 960m.
Starting point: Cerbi, 1420m. At the southern entrance to the village of Esterri d'Àneu turn off right at the place name sign (signpost indicating several places of which 'Serbi' is one). Just before Cerbi you can park on the roadway which goes off to the right with the sign for Estany de la Gola.
Walking times: Cerbi – Estany de la Gola 2¼ hrs.; return 2 hrs.; total time 4¼ hrs.
Height difference: 829m.
Grade: unproblematic walk on a roadway and clear hiking path.
Refreshments: no refreshments along the way; Esterri d'Àneu.

The quiet and little known valley of the Riu d'Unarre is an inviting location for an atmospheric walk. Even if the mountain surroundings with Pic del Ventolau at its centre does not boast very famous names, the beautiful valley and mountain landscape can easily hold its own with the bigger attractions in the nearby national park.

10 minutes along the roadway you come to a signposted junction before **Cerbi** where you continue right. A pretty valley spreads out on the left below with fenced pastures and the Bordes d'Aurós; in early summer the hillsides covered in yellow gorse are striking. The roadway runs across the right hand slope of the valley and as you gain height, look back at the view of the mountains around St. Maurici. After a lengthy stretch up a steady incline the valley gets narrower and the stream cascades down over small ledges. The path starts up round some bends and negotiates the narrow ledge. After that it runs gradu-

ally up the valley and gets closer to the Riu d'Unarre. Cross the stream over the wooden bridge and head towards a valley above which you reach the Planell de Sartari, a pretty area of pastureland criss-crossed by minor streams. Cross the plain where the head of the valley consists of the beautifully stepped waterfall of the Riu d'Unarre. When you reach the waterfall cross over the stream on a little bridge made of logs and now take the obvious path which turns up to the left onto the slope and winds its way up the right hand side of the stream.

Accompanied by the dramatic peaks of the Serra Mitjana in the west, make your way up the very steep head of the valley and then the path changes back onto the other side of the valley and you eventually reach your destination, the **Estany de la Gola**, 2249m.

View down the valley into the mountains of the national park.

Vall de Cardós and Vall de Ferrera

Both of the valleys in the northern Pallars Sobirà push far into the Pyrenean main ridge and are cut off by the central mountain range. No through road connects the valleys with neighbouring France and only a few relatively good and easily accessible mountain passes like Port de Tavascan, Port de Boet or Portella de Baiau allow you to hook up with the French Ariège and Andorra on foot. The natural mountain barrier has managed to preserve until today a pleasant remoteness and tranquility in the valleys and this is especially noticeable in the narrow and dramatic Vall de Ferrera. The 'largest' villages of Alins and Àreu are small tranquil places with a picturesque appearance with well-maintained houses built out of dark slate and are well maintained. A long roadway starts beyond Àreu and leads through the totally enclosed valley which is densely covered with trees. It ends just before the Pla de Boet, a delightful high plain with meadows and side streams in the open valley. A footpath taking a quarter of an hour from the end of the track brings you to the small Refugi Vallferrera, dating back to 1935. This is the first mountain hut to be built in the Catalonian Pyrenees and today marks the starting point for the classic and popular ascent onto Pica d'Estats.

Pica d'Estats – the magical peak of the Vall de Ferrera! At 3143m it is the highest mountain of the Catalonian Pyrenees and already a landmark, but over and over again the broad massif draws your attention from far around with its majestic appearance. The sight of it is particularly imposing in early summer when isolated patches of snow accentuate the shape of this beautiful gigantic rock. There are routes of varying difficulty up to the summit, some from the adjoining French Vallée de Soulcem, but all of them are very demanding in terms of technique and fitness. The surrounding area of Pica d'Estats is formed from glaciers in the most striking way. Numerous lakes lie in the hollows of the imposing circle of mountains carved out from the ice masses which, more or less at an altitude of 3000m, stretches from Pic de Baborte as far as the Canalbona peaks. From this mountain basin a narrow glacial tongue pushed through the Ferrera valley and defined its present shape. It was strengthened by southern glacial inlets which flowed down from the smaller mountain basins. One of them, the Circ de Baiau on the border with Andorra, offers a complete hiking experience within its enchanting landscape without venturing onto a summit.

Iron ore has given its name to Vall de Ferrera. The reddish colour of the stone, particularly around the Monteixo mountains, makes for considerable deposits of ore. Until the end of the 19th century they were worked and processed in the forges of Alins, Àreu and Ainet de Besan. Today there is hardly anything left from the old workshops.

Vall de Cardós runs more openly and broadly in the west with side-valleys

Typical village in the Vall de Ferrera.

which branch off on both sides. You get a magnificent view of the structure of the valley with the numerous little villages from the Serra Mitjana to the west of the main valley which is crossed by the GR11 at the Coll de Jou. You can take a leisurely walk along the crest with fantastic views of the mountains and valley. The main valley divides at Tavascan, the last place with tourist facilities. The road continues to the north to the Pleta del Prat at a height of a good 1700m with the only ski lift in the whole of the area. The walk begins from here onto the inconspicuous mountain of Campirme which, however, has enthralling views of the mountains. Thanks to the road, the efforts of a drive there are minimal, in contrast to the track along the Río Noguera de Lladorre which makes accessible the wonderful lakes at the foot of the border ridge. The currently very bumpy track which is blocked off half way up, forces you into a long hike, combined with an overnight stop in the hut, to the largest lake in the Pyrenees, the Estany de Certascan. This enormous mountain lake is surrounded by a magnificent range of mountains, dominated by the easily climbable Pic de Certascan, but unfortunately it lies too far away for an easy day's walk.

22 Estany del Diable, 2320m, and Pic de Campirme, 2633m

Panoramic mountain with an intermediary stop at the 'devil's lake'

Refugi de la Pleta del Prat – Estany del Diable – Pic de Campirme and back

Location: Tavascan, 1120m.
Starting point: Refugi de la Pleta del Prat, 1720m. From Tavascan along the road to the Estació d'esqui / Pleta del Prat.
Walking times: Refugi de la Pleta del Prat – Estany del Diable 2 hrs.; Estany del Diable – Pic de Campirme 1 hr.; return 2¾ hrs.; total time 5¾ hrs.

Height difference: 913m.
Grade: a technically easy walk; red waymarkings in places and cairns.
Refreshments: Refugi de la Pleta del Prat; Tavascan.
Tip: even without the ascent up to Pic de Campirme this is a very worthwhile walk as regards the scenery.

In summer as in winter the Estany del Diable and Pic de Campirme are a favourite and delightful destination for a walk. While the small 'devil's lake' is protected by pretty mountain ranges of moderate height, Pic de Campirme is open on all sides and offers an excellent panoramic view.

An old roadway starts at the **Refugi** with signposts to your destinations. Follow this roadway for a few minutes until you come to a large wooden signpost where you take the hiking path that branches off to the right. It immediately climbs up across densely overgrown hillsides keeping on the right of the Torrent de Mascarida. At times the path is rather overgrown with thick undergrowth but it soon becomes obvious again. It gets closer to the

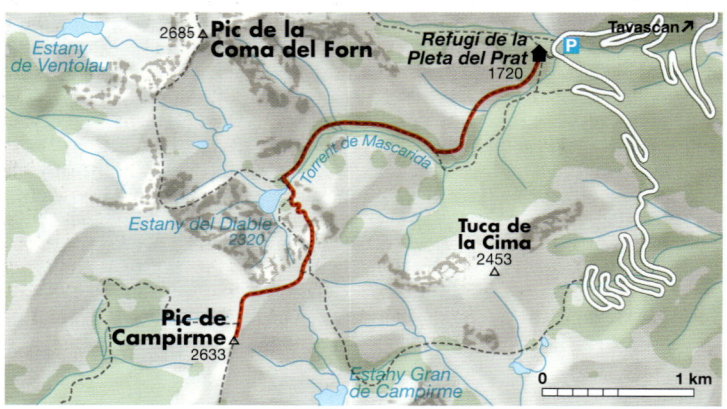

Estany del Diable.

stream, runs beside it for a while, turns off southwestwards and ascends a slope covered in alpine roses. The stream appears again afterwards and your path keeps on the right of it and up a gentle incline reaches a flat area of the valley where you walk past some ruins of huts and a still intact shepherd's hut. Continue along beside the stream which drops down over lovely ledges of moss-covered stones. The path begins to ascend once more and winds up round sharp bends over the head of the valley and in the last seconds brings you unexpectedly to the **Estany del Diable**, 2320m.

At the lake cross over the out-flowing stream. The small grassy col which you are now heading for can clearly be seen in the south east. Take the path which leads across the sloping meadows, but which soon disappears and follow the red paint waymarkings on the rocks. You soon meet some tracks again and after that a conspicuous zigzag path that runs up the broken hillside to the col. Continue to the right along the ridge in a south-southwesterly direction (you could also stay on the edge of the steep slopes dropping down to the lake) and head towards the top of the long-drawn-out ridge. When you reach the top turn southwards with the 'summit' clearly identified by a geodetic sign and arrive directly at the summit of **Pic de Campirme**, 2633m, which is surrounded by derelict defensive walls and little huts.

23 Estanys de Sottlo, 2345m, and d'Estats, 2465m

A walk in front of the high mountain backdrop of Pica d'Estats

Vall Ferrera – Estany de Sottlo – Estany d'Estats and back

Location: Àreu, 1230m.
Starting point: car park in Vall Ferrera, 1790m. From Àreu about 10.5km along the drivable track into Vall Ferrera as far as the car park at the barrier before Pla de Boet.
Walking times: Vall Ferrera – Estany de Sottlo 2¾ hrs.; Estany de Sottlo – Estany d'Estats ½ hr.; return 2¾ hrs.; total time 6 hrs.
Height difference: 675m.
Grade: long walk demanding fitness along clear paths. Waymarked with cairns.
Refreshments: Refugi de Vallferrera, Àreu.

Spring in the valley of the Barranc de Sottlo.

Pica d'Estats – the highest mountain in Catalonia and swathed in characteristic myths! You do not climb on top, instead you only approach the massif as far as the lake of the same name with the imposing south face towering more than 500m above. This beautiful and varied walk follows the normal route to the foot of the climb to the summit.

From the car park in **Vall Ferrera** go a few steps along the roadway and then turn left onto the hiking path which leads to the nearby Refugi de Vallferrera. In front of the hut the signposted path for Pica d'Estats climbs steeply up the hillside in a roughly northerly direction. Keep left at the following fork (right goes to the Estany d'Areste). After that the path turns to the north west and for a while heads out of the valley with a magnificent view of Vall Ferrera before turning into the valley of the Barranc de Sottlo. You walk high above the valley with clear views and then in-between you cross over smallish ledges on the slope with a bit of scrambling until you come to a wooden plank over the valley stream. From now on the path keeps close to the stream along the left hand side at first and heads towards a rocky ledge with pretty waterfalls. The valley ahead is divided into several ledges with small steps in-between cut into the rock which are easily negotiated as you make your way to a last incline up the hillside after a large signpost which brings you to the **Estany de Sottlo**, 2345m. The beautifully embedded lake comes into view unexpectedly and in the background the majestic rock face of Pica d'Estats.

The path continues along the left hand shore. On the north side of the lake it crosses the stream flowing from the area around Pic de Baborte in the west and then keeps to the left of the stream as it ascends once more a grassy, then rocky ledge up to the **Estany d'Estats**, 2465m.

24 Port de Boet, 2509m

Panoramic path onto a French border pass

Vall Ferrera – Port de Boet and back

Location: Àreu, 1230m.
Starting point: car park in Vall Ferrera, 1790m. From Àreu about 10.5km along the drivable track into Vall Ferrera as far as the car park at the barrier before Pla de Boet.
Walking times: Vall Ferrera – Port de Boet 2 hrs.; return 1¾ hrs.; total time 3¾ hrs.
Height difference: 719m.
Grade: technically easy walk on ARP; waymarkings with yellow and black circles.
Refreshments: Refugi de Vallferrera (20 minutes from the car park; path with signpost), Àreu.
Alternative: Pica Roja, 2902m. Excellent panoramic mountain with views of Pica d'Estats, Pic de Sottlo, the French Soulcem valley and Andorra's mountain ranges. The ascent follows the border ridge in a northwesterly direction alternating with steeper sections up a precipitous incline. Under normal conditions no outstandingly technical difficulties, but with a total height variation of 1112m this walk demands fitness!
Time there and back from Port de Boet: 2½ hrs.

An enjoyable walk par excellence. Green mountain pastures with lively streams, high mountain basin surrounded by strikingly formed peaks, a gentle pass with beautiful views and a pleasant path in a little known corner of Vall Ferrera – what more could you want? Perhaps the challenging climb to Pica Roja with its peak of red rock to the northwest of the valley pass?

At the car park in **Vall Ferrera** go past the barrier and continue along the roadway to Pla de Boet, a green high plateau with numerous streamlets and islands of trees in front of an imposing mountain backdrop. At the signpost to Port de Boet turn left from the roadway and cross the plain in the direction of Cabana de Boet. The well marked path runs from there up across a gentle incline of south facing slopes. Barranc d'Arcalis is below you on the right.

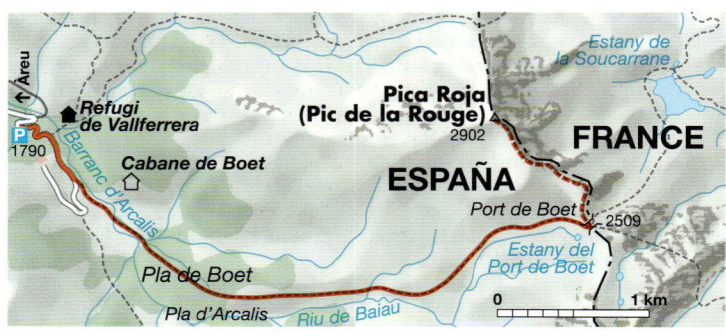

Pla de Boet – idyllic valley plain at the end of Vall Ferrera.

The path continues eastwards without interruption as the view increasingly opens up the mountain basins in the south, especially of the large Circ de Baiau with a pretty plain in front. In the east the Serreta dels Lavans attracts your attention with the prominent peak of the same name. It stands out in the mountain range because of its uniform pyramid shape and is one of the most beautiful mountains in Catalonia.

The path slowly turns northeastwards and then heads for the pass which is just coming into view. Ascending the gentle inclines of the hillside, it goes just before the col on the left past the small Estany del Port de Boet. Another few vertical metres and you are standing on the **Port de Boet**, 2509m, at the pass into Vallée de Soulcem.

25 Estanys de Baiau, 2480m

High mountain lakes in front of a magnificent circle of mountains

Vall Ferrera – Estanys de Baiau and back

Location: Àreu, 1230m.
Starting point: car park in Vall Ferrera, 1790m. From Àreu about 10.5km along the reasonable track into Vall Ferrera as far as the car park at the barrier before Pla de Boet.
Walking times: Vall Ferrera – Estanys de Baiau 2¾ hrs.; return 2¼ hrs.; total time 5 hrs.
Height difference: 690m.
Grade: walk without any particular problems along the GR11.
Refreshments: Ref. de Vallferrera (20 mins. from the car park; path signposted); Àreu.
Tip: Refugi de Baiau: good self-catering hut for 12 people.

Alternative: Coll dels Estanys Forcats, 2740m. Nearby border pass to Andorra with impressive views. From the Refugi de Baiau descend eastwards to the north side of the lake, there turn uphill onto the west-facing grassy hillside. The path narrows as it ascends to a small sloping ledge in front of which you cross diagonally left to the stream and then on the right of it with clear tracks, you ascend the valley. The pass soon comes into view, the valley runs gradually uphill where the slopes are totally covered in boulders. Keeping to the valley floor you arrive at the pass without any problems. Time there and back from the Refugi de Baiau: 1½ hrs.

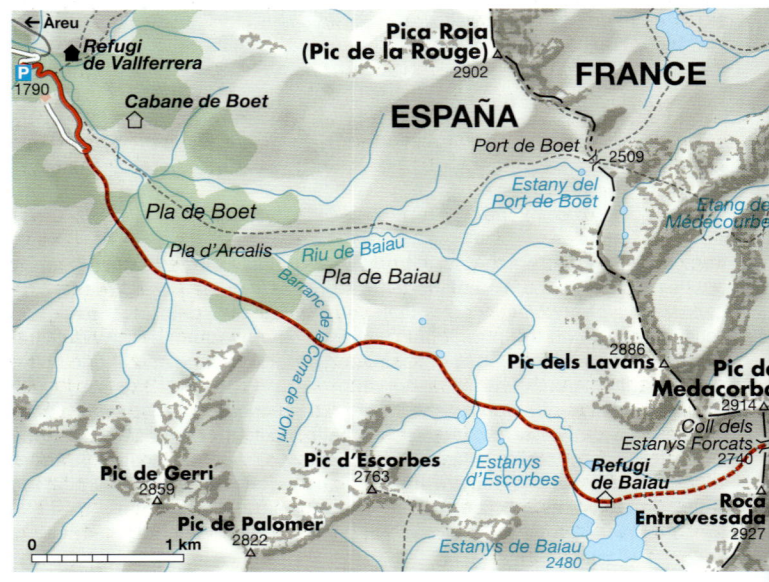

The delightful valley plain of Pla de Boet forms the starting point for an exciting and scenically diverse walk to the southernmost end of Vall Ferrera. The glacially defined Circ de Baiau with its pretty lakes is surrounded by an imposing rock face which seals it off from the neighbouring Andorra. Two high passes allow you to cross over into Andorra and the pass suggested in the alternative provides you with a breathtaking view.

From the car park in **Vall Ferrera** walk along the roadway to the Pla de Boe where a signpost also indicates the Circ de Baiau. A few paces further on the GR path turns off left from the roadway, stays above the valley floor across hillsides covered in meadow flowers and then quickly ascends up to Pla d'Arcalis.

Pica Roja as you look down through the valley.

Continue close to the stream across the hillside covered with individual pines and birch trees and afterwards the path ascends once more across wooded slopes. You get closer to the stream again. Alternating short inclines with more level ground the path then goes from one tiny valley into the next until you come to a wide valley that is crossed by the branching meanders of the Barranc de la Coma de l'Orri.

Cross over the stream and go round the Pic d'Escorbes which extends northwards and beyond the foothills turn into the Baiau valley. Pica Roja attracts your attention in the north and the beautifully formed pyramid of Pic dels Lavans opposite. Your path leads a long way across the valley floor in a succession of comfortable inclines and over gentle hills. The Refugi de Baiau on a rocky knoll soon becomes visible at the foot of the mountain basin at the head of the valley. At the Estanys d'Escorbes you come to some pastureland, cross the out-flowing stream and walk past the lakes on the left hand side. Ascending more again, the path heads towards the stream from the Estanys de Baiau, pushes on up the slope and gets to the top of the sheer drop. After that you arrive at the smaller of the **Estanys de Baiau**, 2480m, and cross the out-flowing stream. At the foot of the rocky hill on which the refuge lies you reach the north and west side of the big Baiau lake. A short climb brings you to the refuge and from there you can descend again to its eastern side.

26 Ermita St. Miquel, 1200m, and Besan, 1160m

Quiet excursion to an abandoned mountain village

Bordes de Felip – St. Miquel – Besan and back

Location: Alins, 1040m.
Starting point: Bordes de Felip, 950m. The farmstead lies on the L-510 at km 5 from Llavorsí in the direction of Alins. Park at the old road sign for Besan 0.8 km.
Walking times: Bordes de Felip – St. Miquel 1 hr.; St. Miquel – Besan ¼ hr.; return 1 hr.; total time 2¼ hrs.

Height difference: 250m.
Grade: short easy walk on an old bridle path; in places faded blue and orange waymarkings.
Refreshments: none along the way; Alins.
Tip: out of respect for the inhabitants, please take the path described here and not the one leading through the farm land.

Ermita St. Miquel.

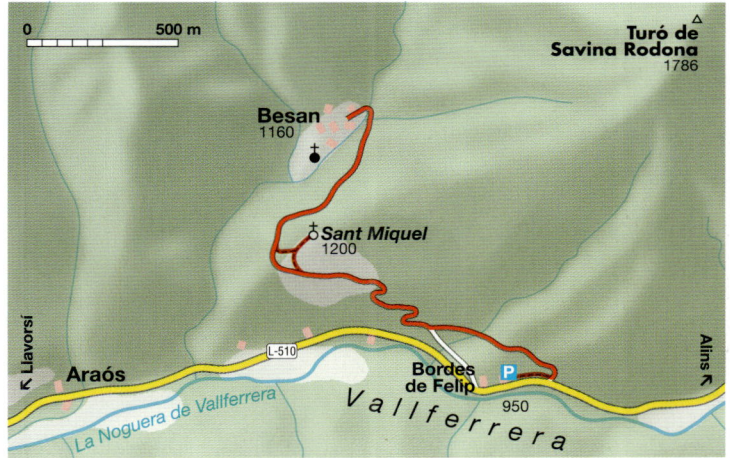

The story of the remote mountain village of Besan is typical of the fate of many Pyrenean villages. Its inhabitants held out until the 70s – without electric light, only connected by a bridle path to the main valley and living off the land. The village has been abandoned and is slowly crumbling apart as it stands in conflicting contrast to its pretty surroundings. The nearby chapel of St. Miquel which you pass by on this walk, is an attractive place to stop for a picnic on a mild summer's evening.

At **Bordes de Felip** follow the large signpost for Sant Miquel and go along the old broken road in the direction of the water pipe. Just beforehand a path goes off in the opposite direction and runs across hillsides of holm oak trees until it joins with the bridle path coming in from the left.

From here, waymarked with paint, the cleverly constructed and reinforced path ascends the steep slope above the valley and eventually leads onto grassy sloping terraces where the waymarkings get a little lost. Just go straight up over the terraces to a signpost that indicates left to Besan. The detour to the chapel goes to the right. The narrow path runs in a northeasterly direction and after a few minutes reaches the Ermita **St. Miquel**, 1200m, from where you can already see the roofs of Besan. Follow the signpost back on the main path and you meet a shady path down to the stream and a wooden plank which leads across to **Besan**, 1160m.

Andorra

You can enjoy a sensational panoramic view on Pic de Coma Pedrosa, the highest peak in Andorra (Walk 27).

A short visit to this tax haven and consumer paradise between Spain and France will leave you with barely any other impression than being cramped, noisy, dreadfully overdeveloped and overrun with traffic. The dense occupation of the principality is concentrated in the central valley along the Riu Valira d'Orient which forms the connection between Spain and France. One resort follows another, or you could say that the capital of Andorra la Vella is extending more and more along the narrow valley. Is Andorra a walker's paradise? The question deserves an unreserved 'yes', since there are some quiet and undeveloped valleys that branch off directly from the main through road and lead into the most superb mountainous regions. If, when you get to Soldeu, you turn off into Vall d'Incles or Vall de Ransol, you will immediately notice the stark contrast between the busy central axis of Andorra and the assorted attractions of its mountains. This is particularly noticeable in the western central valley along the Riu Valira del Nord where, to the north of Ordino after just a few kilometres, the towns become smaller and you experience a more peaceful and unexpected tranquility and remoteness amongst the most impressive mountain scenery.

Distances in Andorra are given to the decimal point. With a surface area of only 464km2 Andorra combines the diversity of the Pyrenean landscape in the smallest space. At the same time it is home to a concentration of deep and long valleys like Vall de Madriu, superbly shaped mountain basins like the Circ dels Pessons and sparse summits like Pic de la Serrera. Nor should we forget the delightful mountain lakes and streams. There are, of course, the ski complexes too which bestow on Andorra a vigorous winter tourism and considerably distinguish many of the mountains. But in most cases you only brush against them at the start of the walk to then quickly lose them from sight.

The highest peak in Andorra is Pic de Coma Pedrosa, at 2942m just under the 3000m mark, and it is entirely within Andorran boundaries. This lends an extra distinction to the not especially noteworthy mountain in the eyes of many local people which it deserves, in fact, more for its fabulous wide panoramic views. For this reason, Pic de Casamanya, a more modest peak as regards height, is said to be the mountain with the best views in Andorra. It is situated between the two Valira valleys in the centre of the country, offers a brilliant view of the beautiful mountain ranges and valleys of this small state, which are stacked up one behind the other and which promise a variety of enjoyable walks.

In Vall de Madriu (Walk 36).

27 Refugi de Coma Pedrosa, 2272m, and Pic de Coma Pedrosa, 2942m

Not a mountain in its actual shape, but a first class peak for the views it offers

Arinsal – Aigües Juntes – Refugi de Coma Pedrosa – Estany Negre – Pic de Coma Pedrosa and back

Location: Arinsal, 1480m.
Starting point: Arinsal, small car park at the Torrent Ribal, 1580m. In Arinsal first go in the direction of Estació d'Esqui d'Arinsal, but at the turn-off to the ski station go straight ahead through a tunnel to the end of the road at the channelled Torrent Ribal.
Walking times: Arinsal – Aigües Juntes ¾ hr.; Aigües Juntes – Refugi de Coma Pedrosa 1½ hrs.; Refugi de Coma Pedrosa – Estany Negre 1¼ hrs.; Estany Negre – Pic de Coma Pedrosa 1 hr.; return 3¾ hrs.; total time 8-9 hrs.
Height difference: 1362m.
Grade: very long summit ascent with an emphasis on good fitness. The incline of the ridge has some steep sections. As far as Estany Negre GR path, then yellow waymarkers and cairns.
Refreshments: Ref. de Coma Pedrosa; Arinsal.
Tip: thanks to the staffed hut half way along the route, you can take two days to complete this walk.

Luxuriant meadows of flowers, lively waterfalls and dense woods accompany the ascent through the valley of Riu de Coma Pedrosa which was one of the most unspoiled in the region until the building of the mountain hut. From the refuge you climb onto the highest mountain of the principality which Andorrans make a lot of fuss about because they do not have to share it with any of their neighbours! The key point is, however, the brilliant far-reaching views in all directions.

At **Arinsal** car park pick up the track which leads away from the Torrent Ribal immediately after a bend. Follow the track past a barrier until you come to a right hand bend with a signpost where your hiking path turns off left. This takes you into the valley of the Riu de Coma Pedrosa and ascends through a pine wood to the **Aigües Juntes**, 1760m, the confluence of the Riu d'Areny and

On the summit ridge.

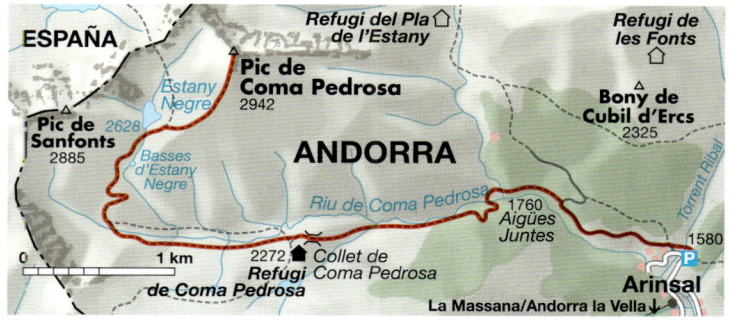

the valley stream. Cross both of the streams, one after the other, on little bridges. The path now winds steeply up on the left hand side of the Riu de Coma Pedrosa onto flatter ground and you can see beautiful waterfalls further ahead. With a varying gradient the path crosses hillsides where trees give way increasingly to dense rhododendron bushes. As the big waterfall disappears out of sight on your right, the path runs up through a green landscape of streams and at the bottom of a small valley you then cross over the stream coming from the Estany de les Truites and ascend steeply again up the right hand slope to the Collet de Coma Pedrosa before the extensive high plain through which the stream runs. The path turning off left leads to the nearby **Refugi de Coma Pedrosa**, 2272m, while straight on continues to Pic de Coma Pedrosa. Descend to the valley floor, go past a sign for Estany Negre and cross over the wide plain on the left of the stream. You can see ahead the abrupt head of the valley with Pic de Sanfonts in the centre and on the right ahead a broad waterfall coming from the Riu de l'Estany. After gentle grassy slopes to start with the path gets steeper and comes into a little valley where it stays on the left of the stream at first, then changes over onto the other side where it ascends some sharp bends and further up crosses over the Riu de l'Estany. Go past a small lake on the right, the Basses d'Estany Negre, ascend the following narrow valley of scree up to the junction of paths for the Port de Baiau, which is where the GR now heads, and Pic de Coma Pedrosa. Your destination is indicated with yellow paint on a boulder and you leave the GR here to the right and follow the yellow marked path that climbs up the scree. It rises above the **Estany Negre**, 2628m, and climbs up to the southwest hump of the mountain ridge. Follow the line of the ridge with varying degrees of steepness. After the path goes at first along the right of the crest and has then crossed onto the left hand side, there follows a short final spurt and you are standing on the top of **Pic de Coma Pedrosa**, 2942m.

28 Through the Circ de Tristaina, 2500m

High mountain trail between peaks and lakes

Coma del Forat – Estany del Mig – Estany de Més Amunt – Coma del Forat

Location: El Serrt, 1540m.
Starting point: Coma del Forat, car park at the Estació d'esqui Ordino Arcalís, 2220m.
Walking times: Coma del Forat – Estany del Mig ¾ hr.; Estany del Mig – north side of Estany de Més Amunt ¾ hr.; north side of Estany de Més Amunt – Coma del Forat 1½ hrs.; total time 3 hrs.
Height difference: 280m.
Grade: technically easy mountain trail up steep hillsides with rock slopes; yellow waymarkers.
Refreshments: restaurant in the ski lift area; el Serrat.
Alternative: return via Estany Primer, 2250m. At the Estany del Mig cross the out-flowing stream again and stay on its left hand side down the valley to the Estany Primer. Continue along the flat shoreline path to the end of the lake where the out-flowing stream is immediately crossed. After that, ascend a little (yellow waymarker) to a hill on the slope and then descend once more to the valley stream (Riu de Tristaina). Cross over on some logs then ascend to the road where you come out at a signpost and a stone with the inscription in white for the 'Llacs' somewhere between the O-shaped sculpture and Coma del Forat. Walking time from Estany del Mig: ½ hr. Also possible as an alternative approach.

The Circ de Tristaina and the mountain lakes surrounded by it in the north west of Andorra are the destination for this walk which keeps predominantly between mountain top and valley bottom. On the precipitous slopes of the mountain range there's a beautiful and exciting circular walk which constantly opens up new perspectives of the two lakes and the mountain basin dominated by Pic de Tristaina.

From the car park at the **Coma de Forat** proceed to Restaurant La Coma. Go past it on the right and a few metres uphill to a path crossing the slope. Follow this path to the right and climb up to a small col beyond which the Circ de Tristaina opens up. Go past a pond on the left hand side down to the stream from the **Estany del Mig**, 2290m, cross over some stones to the other side and continue a short way along the path close to the shore.

Afterwards change onto the yellow marked hiking path which ascends the slope of the shore and climbs above the large Estany de Més Amunt. Continue at first along the right of the stream and, just before a largish heap of stones on the other side of the stream, the path turns off to the left (marked yellow), crosses the stream and now heads towards the steep hillsides which slope down to the lake. Ascending some bends you reach the highest point of the circular walk above the north side of the **Estany de Més Amunt**, 2500m. Now with a lot of ups-and-downs, again and again over rocks and boulders, continue through the precipitous hillsides high above the lakes. After you have negotiated a sheer drop on the western side of the circle of mountains you come past a small viewing platform with a decorative stone tower. Here you are afforded stunning views of the lakes and the mountain basin. The path now descends steadily down the hillside and reaches your outward path near the col. From here continue back to the car park.

Circ de Tristaina with the peak of the same name on the right.

29 Pic de Tristaina, 2878m

Border summit with brilliant views

Coma del Forat – Estany del Mig – Tristaina-Pass – Pic de Tristaina and back

Location: El Serrat, 1540m.
Starting point: Coma del Forat, car park at the Estació d'esqui Ordino Arcalís, 2220m.
Walking times: Coma del Forat – Estany del Mig ¾ hr.; Estany del Mig – Tristaina-Pass 1 hr.; Tristaina-Pass – Pic de Tristaina ½ hr.; return 2 hrs.; total time 4¼ hrs.
Height difference: 658m.
Grade: summit walk with a very steep pass followed by a ridge ascent with easy sections of climbing up to Grade 1.
Refreshments: restaurant in the ski lift area; el Serrat.

In the circle of mountains named after it, Pic de Tristaina is the highest and also most beautiful peak. Due to the landscape of lakes at its foot and the magnificent panoramic views from the top it is a popular destination, from the French side as well as from the Andorran side. The ridge incline is well marked but requires you to do a bit of climbing. However you can make it easier by going round it on the slope.

From the car park at the **Coma Forat** first follow the previous Walk 28. At the yellow marked turn-off to the left keep going along the right hand side of the stream for another 20 metres until you come to the pile of stones and then cross the stream (be careful here: the more obvious path which goes out from the small lakes situated a bit higher up, leads to the Port de l'Arbella!). At first an inconspicuous path, then a really obvious one marked with cairns, runs through the grassy terrain and heads in a north-northeasterly direction towards the gap on the right below Pic de Tristaina. It later runs up the broken and increasingly steep slope – cairns make up for the unclear stretches of path which also lead through a small boulder field – and gets closer to the narrow gap. At a small levelling off on the slope up to the pass, about 30 vertical metres below the gap, cairns indicate the alternative path going off left. This leads onto the mountain hillside of Pic de Tristaina, ascends steeply there – well-trodden and copiously waymarked – and reaches the flat ridge at a large cairn a few metres west of the summit. Climb up to the **Tristaina pass**, 2694m, and turn to the left. First go round the ridge of boulders on the left hand side, then the easily visible path keeps directly on the rocky ridge for a while, swings again out to the left and climbs a less steep broken flank. Continue there in an almost direct line up to the flat summit ridge, go a few steps along to the left until you reach **Pic de Tristaina**, 2878m.

Ascent to Pic de Tristaina.

30 Estany Blau, 2335m

Via the Port de Siguer to the 'blue lake'

La Rabassa – Refugi de Rialb – Port de Siguer – Estany Blau and back

Location: El Serrat, 1540m.
Starting point: La Rabassa, 1780m, car park at the end of the road into Valle de Sorteny. The signposted road soon turns off right after Serrat.
Walking times: La Rabassa – Refugi de Rialb 1 hr.; Refugi de Rialb – Port de Siguer 1¼ hrs.; Port de Siguer – Estany Blau ½ hr.; return 2¼ hrs.; total time 5 hrs.
Height difference: 615m.
Grade: altogether easy walk on yellow marked paths, although the ascent up to the Port de Siguer is really steep.
Refreshments: no opportunities along the way; el Serrat.
Tip: Refugi de Rialb: self-catering hut for 6 to 10 people.

The walk is more like a pleasant stroll in the pretty valley of the Riu Rialb as you go along beside the lively stream and across broad green hillsides. Some effort is needed on the ascent up to the Siguer pass before you are able to enjoy the magnificent view of the surrounding mountains on the French side and of the Estany Blau which resembles a piece of mounted jewellery. The lake appears to shine in varying tones of blue depending on the amount of light.

Right at the start of **La Rabassa** car park keep left according to the information board where you follow the signpost for Portella de Rialb. The path goes through a shady picnic area, then gently ascends on the right hand side of the pretty stream and runs through the widening valley. Go past the **Refugi de Rialb**, 1990m, on the right of the path and situated a little higher up, cross the stream on a metal bridge, keep on its left hand side for a while and come to a fork where the Estany Blau is indicated in yellow on a rock. Cross over onto the right hand side again on a metal bridge and continue parallel to the stream first, turn off right before the Cabana dels Planells de

A few metres on the French side – Estany Blau.

Rialb. The end of the valley with the towering Pic de Font Blanca can now be seen easily. The path ascends the slope, runs past the stone hut at some distance and swings onto the slope of the pass. Ascend steeply up a zigzag path to the flatter incline of the hillside and go across this to the **Port de Siguer**, 2395m, which is guarded by a large cairn.

The half-hidden Estany Blau lies on the right below the pass. Descend the yellow marked path a short way and after a cattle gate continue on the level along the slope, then ascend again to climb round a protrusion. The path finally descends quickly down the hillside. Past a rock-strewn slope it then goes across meadowed slopes down to the **Estany Blau**, 2335m, and the out-flowing stream. From there you can take a pleasant walk along the left hand shore.

31 Vall de Sorteny and Pic de la Serrera, 2913m

A picture-book valley of flowers and an excellent summit for views

La Rabassa – Refugi de Sorteny – Collada dels Meners – Pic de la Serrera and back

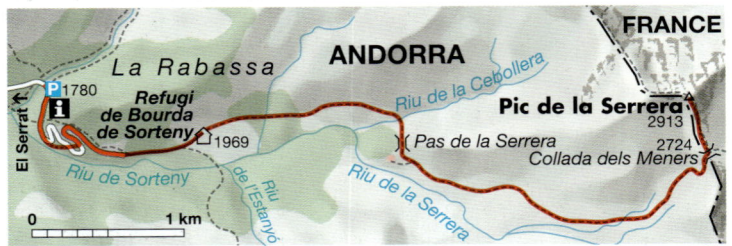

Location: El Serrat, 1540m.
Starting point: La Rabassa, 1780m (for access see Walk 30). You can drive along the track as far as the Portell de Sorteny, 1880m, up until 10 o'clock.
Walking times: La Rabassa – Refugi de Sorteny ½ hr.; Refugi de Sorteny – Collada dels Meners 2¼ hrs.; Collada dels Meners – Pic de la Serrera ¾ hr.; return 3 hrs.; total time 6½ hrs.
Height difference: 1133m.

Grade: moderately difficult, long walk with a large variation in height; steep gradient on the summit ascent. Yellow and red marked path as far as the Collada dels Meners; after that rather confusing yellow, then red waymarkings, but always clear tracks.
Refreshments: no opportunities along the way; el Serrat.
Tip: Refugi de Sorteny: large self-catering hut for 30 people.

Because of its unique abundance of flowers Vall de Sorteny was declared a national park in 1999. The walk through the valley is not only a botanical experience, it also offers some scenic delights culminating in the superb panoramic views from Pic de la Serrera. It's also worth mentioning that the walk is just as rewarding even without making a summit ascent.
At the car park of **La Rabassa** go to the Parc Natural de la Vall de Sorteny information board and take the track there up to the first left hand bend. Turn right here along one of the Senderos botánicos which serves as a shortcut. The path follows the contours of the mountains and first ascends up beside the stream. It crosses the track further up, ascends some steps and meets the track once more. Follow it here to the left and afterwards go past a small botanical garden and on to the Portell de Sorteny where the track ends. The hiking path starts here and runs through a pretty landscape of streams, past

a right hand turn-off to the Estany de l'Estanyó (see Walk 32) to the **Refugi de Sorteny**, 1969m. Go on the left past the hut and across dense slopes of flowers, through a light stand of pines and many blossoming meadows. The path slowly begins to ascend and heads up the hillside, then changes over to the other side of the stream and now winds away from the stream steeply up the right hand slope of the valley to the Pas de la Serrera. The small col forms the crossing between the valley of the Riu de la Cebollera and that of the Riu de la Serrera. You come into a beautiful high valley with flower-covered meadows and a lovely meandering stream beyond which the path now leads up to the pass. On the hillside it swings diagonally left and then zigzags steeply up onto the col. During the ascent you are afforded good views of the huge broad Pic de la Serrera.

On the **Collada dels Meners**, 2724m, (marked Coll de la Mina when you are there) leave the yellow and red marked path which descends into Valle de Ransol. Turn to the left following an obvious path and stay at first on the right below the rocky ridge, then on the broad grassy crest of the ridge. As soon as it gets narrower and rockier the gradient becomes much steeper and your path runs round narrow bends and steeply up to the level summit of **Pic de la Serrera**, 2913m.

Destination reached – summit of Pic de la Serrera.

32 Estany de l'Estanyó, 2340m

Secluded lake surrounded by large mountains

La Rabassa – Estret de l'Estanyó – Estany de l'Estanyó and back

Location: El Serrat, 1540m.
Starting point: La Rabassa, 1780m. For access see Walk 30.
Walking times: La Rabassa – Estret de l'Estanyó 1¼ hrs.; Estret de l'Estanyó – Estany de l'Estanyó ¾ hr.; return 1½ hrs.; total time 3½ hrs.
Height difference: 560m.
Grade: easy walk on yellow marked paths.
Refreshments: no opportunities along the way; el Serrat.

This lake in a pretty location at the foot of Pic de l'Estanyó, the second highest mountain in Andorra, is an ideal place for a rest and a swim after an enjoyable walk through meadows of flowers, little woods and across gentle slopes.
From the car park of **La Rabassa** to the signposted fork to the Estany de l'Estanyó follow the previous directions in Walk 31. Turn off right and cross over the valley stream on a little bridge. With varying degrees of steepness

The Estanyó lake lies hidden at the foot of the mountains.

At your destination – Estany de l'Estanyó.

the path leads through the most luxuriant meadows full of flowers, light birch and pine trees and across slopes covered in dense rhododendron bushes before it comes out onto open, gently undulating hillsides. In the south you can see the beautifully formed head of the valley of the Serra de l'Estanyó. You come close to the stream and on its right hand side reach a small narrow pass, the **Estret de l'Estanyó**, 2200m, with a wall running right across it which you can either pass through where there's a gate or climb over.

After that begins an area of extensive pastureland where the path moves further away from the stream again and slowly ascends up to a high plain of meadows which it crosses to the south. After going over a stream the path leisurely ascends and heads towards the small incline of the slope after which you arrive at the **Estany de l'Estanyó**, 2340m.

33 Pic de Casamanya, 2740m

The 'magical mountain' in Andorra

Coll d'Ordino – Cap de l'Astrell – Pic de Casamanya and back

Location: Ordino, 1295m.
Starting point: Coll d'Ordino, 1983m. You can drive to the pass from Ordino or Canillo.
Walking times: Coll d'Ordino – Cap de l'Astrell ¾ hr.; Cap de l'Astrell – Pic de Casamanya 1½ hrs.; return 2 hrs.; total time 4¼ hrs.
Height difference: 757m.
Grade: technically easy walk, but with some steep sections; yellow marked path.
Refreshments: no opportunities along the way; Ordino; Canillo.

An elevation like Pic de Casamanya, situated in the centre of the country and with a panoramic view to all sides which gets wider and wider as you ascend to the summit point, would most probably count as a 'magical mountain' in a Latin-American country. It is also a bit magical in Andorra, but the ascent of this peak with wonderful views is, in any case, obligatory.

On the **Coll d'Ordino** the large wooden sign for Casamanya indicates the path which immediately enters a pine wood. At first steeply, then more moderately, the path ascends through the shady wood. You leave the path briefly at the Collada de les Vaques, a clearing on the slope, then walk through another little wood and soon afterwards you come to the **Cap de l'Astrell**, 2175m, where the ground is conspicuously treeless. From here you can look along the line of the bulging south ridge of Casamanya.

The path now follows the elongated ridge alternating between grassy and broken terrain. After a stretch up a comfortable incline there follows a steeper knoll with a steep zigzag path on which you quickly gain height.

On the return from the summit.

The path levels out again and the gentle rise of the summit lies ahead. The path now runs directly up to the top of **Pic de Casamanya**, 2740m.

34 Estanys de Juclar, 2294m, and Coll de l'Alba, 2546m

Through the well-known Vall de Juclar to a pass with beautiful views – and some would say onto the most striking peak in Andorra

Pont de la Baladosa – Refugi de Juclar – Collada de Juclar – Coll de l'Alba and back

Location: Soldeu, 1820m.
Starting point: Pont de la Baladosa, 1850m, at the end of the road into Vall d'Incles. Park before the bridge.
Walking times: Pont de la Baladosa – Refugi de Juclar 1¾ hrs.; Refugi de Juclar – Collada de Juclar ¾ hr.; Collada de Juclar – Coll de l'Alba ¼ hr.; return 2¼ hrs.; total time 5 hrs.
Height difference: 726m.
Grade: not very demanding walk on well-trodden paths; waymarked yellow as far as Collada de Juclar.
Refreshments: bar at the campsite d'Incles; Soldeu.
Tip: Refugi de Juclar, 2320m: comfortable self-catering hut with 30 places.
Alternative: Pic d'Escobes; 2781m. The beautiful and striking peak resembling a leaning tooth of rock p.108 can be seen from many points in Andorra.

The ascent is well-marked with cairns and has very steep sections up to the Coll de Noé as well as some climbing (grade II) to the summit. From the Coll de l'Alba follow the waymarkings and tracks at first in a southerly direction towards the ridge of the col, but then turn diagonally right and continue uphill onto the north-northwest face to reach a 'grassy' long groove which runs down from the Coll de Noé. The small 'col' on the boulder-strewn ridge can be identified by a jutting rock slab which looks like a lopsided chimney from below. The ascent is steep up this groove which becomes rocky as it nears the Coll. From there a path crosses over the slope to a narrow col at the foot of Pic d'Escobes. Climb up the ridge to the airy summit. Total time there and back from the Coll de l'Alba 2½ hrs.

Vall de Juclar.

Vall d'Incles is a quiet oasis in the noisy central valley of Andorra. Your walk begins here along the Riu de Juclar through the densely green valley up to the Estanys de Juclar that lie in a gneiss hollow carved out by glaciers. The smaller of the two lakes at the foot of the pointed Pic d'Escobes is a pretty place to stop for a rest on this walk which ends on the Coll de l'Alba. The pass over to France comes as a pleasant surprise with views of the bordering mountains – and could be a prelude to the ascent of Pic d'Escobes. The summit is an exquisite viewing point.

Cross the **Pont de la Baladosa** and continue along the adjoining track, past the path branching off right to the Basses del Siscaró. The track ends at a little bridge over the stream and there's a picnic area on the other side. Your path goes past this, moves away from the stream and begins the ascent of several steps in the valley, repeatedly getting closer to and then further away from the stream as it does so. With intermittent short level sections of the path, climb up through dense slopes of flowers and rhododendrons and in-between time a wooden plank leads across to the right hand side of the stream. The ascent up the valley ends in the Pleta de Juclar, a grassy high plain criss-crossed with rivulets with individual rocky knolls. The path turns

The alluring Pic d'Escobes, a lopsided tooth of rock, in the background.

Pic d'Escobes – an alternative destination on this walk.

left here and crosses the Pleta and a concrete path leads to the other side of the stream. Near to a rock tunnel used for controlling the out-flowing stream cross over the mostly dry streambed for the last time. Just before the first lake the path divides, both branches – to the left more leisurely, to the right a little steeper – lead to the small dam of Estany Primer de Juclar. Shortly afterwards turn off right according to the sign and climb up the grassy hillside to the **Refugi de Juclar**, 2320m. From there the path leads onto the lakeside slope, runs above the lake to its eastern end and then descends – partly across a slope covered in boulders – to the stretch of land between the two lakes. You reach the western side of Estany Segon de Juclar where you cross the out-flowing stream on a metal bridge and the path now ascends steeply up the sloping shore away from the lake and in a northerly direction onto **Collada de Juclar**, 2442m. The col presents you with a beautiful panoramic view of the lakes. Turn sharply to the right to ascend stony ground at first steeply, then continue more on the level onto the nearby **Coll de l'Alba**, 2546m.

35 Circ dels Pessons and Pic de Gargantillar, 2864m

Lakes – one after the other like a string of pearls

Grau Roig – Estany dels Pessons – Collada dels Pessons – Pic de Gargantillar and back

Location: Soldeu, 1820m.
Starting point: Grau Roig ski station, 2110m; car park west of the Valira d'Orient stream.
Turn off right to the Estació d'Esqui from the road to Port d'Envalira, then go along the road branching off right before the large parking area and over the bridge across the Valira d'Orient to the car park.
Walking times: Grau Roig – Estany dels Pessons ¾ hr.; Estany dels Pessons – Collada dels Pessons 2 hrs.; Collada dels Pessons – Pic de Gargantillar ¼ hr.; return 2¾ hrs.; total time 5¾ hrs.
Height difference: 754m.
Grade: long walk with pleasantly varied inclines, except for the very steep climb up to the Collada dels Pessons. GR 7 path.
Refreshments: restaurant at Estany dels Pessons; Soldeu.

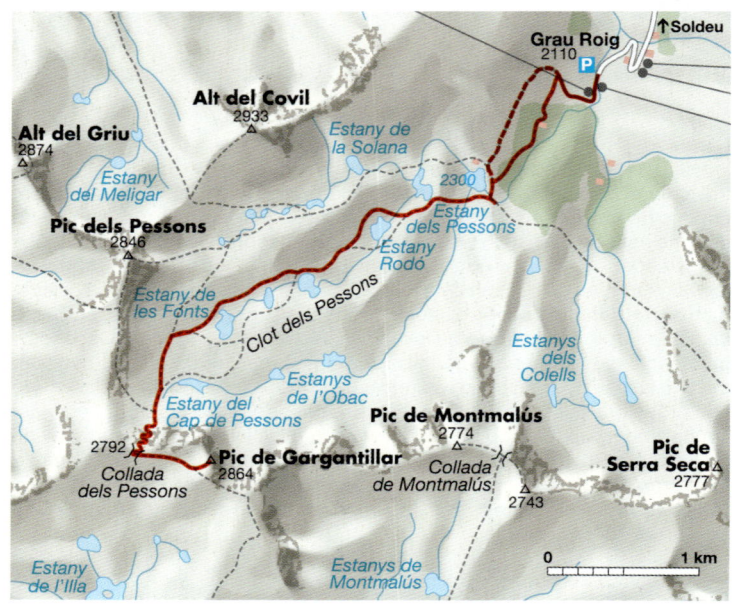

Enchanting lakes in front of Pic de Gargantillar.

Each lake is more enchanting than the next! The hike through the wonderful granite landscape of the Circ dels Pessons with its unusual rock formations is one of the finest walks. The ascent to the towering peak of the cirque is almost an appendage, but only just, since the view from the top encompasses not only the whole ensemble of lakes and pools, but also the important peaks and mountain ranges of eastern Andorra, and extends into the French Carlit massif.

At the car park of **Grau Roig** go back across the bridge, immediately afterwards continue right along the track past two chair lift stations, then follow the track ascending on the right with the sign for the Restaurant del Llac dels Pessons. The track forks again afterwards: either follow it to the first lake or take a shortcut through the wood. In this case continue left, past an artificial ski slope where the track gets narrower. About 50 metres before a stream leave the track and take the path indicated by cairns on the right at the edge of the wood which ascends through the wood and finishes at **Estany dels Pessons**, 2300m. The restaurant lies at the north end of the lake, and you continue left to a large signpost. The Collada del Montmalús is signposted on the left, but your path, marked white and red, sets off to the right. It crosses several side streams and then ascends through meadows and granite boulders to the sedimented Estany Forcat, 2362m, on the left hand side of which you cross the stream.

The path now turns to the southwest and brings the impressive Circ dels Pessons into view. Going past a pond on the left hand side brings you to Estany Rodó, 2374m. The path skirts the lake on the right and then runs up the leisurely incline of grassy and boulder strewn slopes. The rugged face between Pics d'Ensagents and Cubil accompanies you as the view of the Circ dels Pessons with its steep northern faces improves with every step.

At the Estany del Meligar, 2440m, continue on the right of the lake and ascend rapidly, a short way over large boulders. After a small lake you come to Estany de les Fonts, 2489m, with a pond just in front of it. After the lake which has been engulfed with underwater plants the path goes up the hillside ahead and then comes to the foot of the mountain basin. It is covered on the left by a hillside of boulders at the foot of Pic dels Pessons. The path heads for the Collada dels Pessons, keeps going through the debris covered foot of the slope up to the col and then swings onto the grassy flank. The at first long-drawn-out bends become really steep zigzags further up which bring you to the **Collada dels Pessons**, 2792m.

The fantastic view of the valley you have just walked through with its chain of lakes, more than makes up for the strenuous climb. The Pic dels Pessons rises up unmistakably nearby. Turn to the left and follow the path along the line of the ridge. It descends gently at first, then runs up

View back from Pic de Gargantillar.

onto the southwest slope and passes a pre-summit which is separated from the main summit by a steep northern notch. As soon as you have gone past this turn off left from the GR and go up along the edge of the precipice to **Pic de Gargantillar**, 2864m.

36 Vall de Madriu

The most unspoiled valley in Andorras

Escaldes – Refugi de Fontverd – Refugi Riu dels Orris and back

Location: Escaldes, 1053m.
Starting point: CS-101 near km 7, 1230m. At the exit from Escaldes (in the direction of Encamp) take the no. 200 road which branches off right in the direction of Engolasters. After about 1km turn right onto the CS-101 over the bridge of the Riu Madriu. Just afterwards turn off left at the large signposts for Entremesaigües / Camí de la Muntanya of the GR7. It's possible to park at the large building on the right about 300m further along on the road.

Walking times: Starting point – Refugi de Fontverd 1¾ hrs.; Refugi de Fontverd – Refugi Riu dels Orris 2 hrs.; return 3 hrs.; total time 6¾ hrs.
Height difference: 1000m.
Grade: very long walk, steep inclines and large variation in height, but with no technical difficulties. Leisurely GR 7 path all the way.
Refreshments: Escaldes.
Tip: the Refugis de Fontverd and Riu dels Orris are decent self-catering huts with 14 and 10 places respectively.

Solitude and tranquility reign in Vall de Riu Madriu (see photo on p. 91). The longest high valley in Andorra is only accessible along a wonderful hiking path which leads up as far as Estany de l'Illa on the rear side of the Pessons peak. Dense woods, with idyllic meadows in-between, a stream alternating between meanders and seething waterfalls and the steep rocky flanks of the southern side of the valley in the background – a wonderful place for quiet contemplation!

The **GR7**, an old bridle path and reinforced with natural stone, leads you through a mixed forest up to Pont de Sassanat and there onto the other side of the Riu Madriu. Ascending steeply up the winding path through enclosed pastures you come to Entremesaigües, a small group of houses near to the bridge of the same name. At the signposted junction keep straight on in the direction of Estany de l'Illa. Keep ascending and past another fork the valley broadens out and makes room for terraced meadows with a prettily maintained group of houses. This tiny idyllic place is

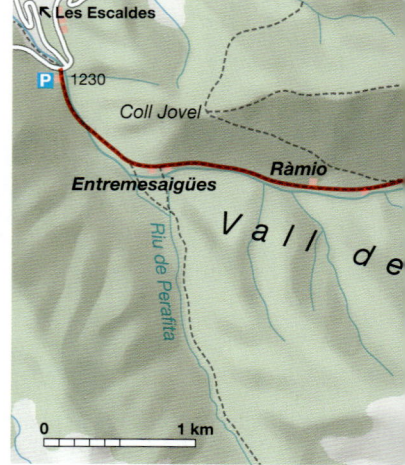

called Ràmio and just beyond on the left the GR11 joins your path which now runs along beside the enclosed pastures and meadows more or less close to the stream. Ignore the signposted turn-off to the Coll de Jovell on the left and with a more clearly increasing gradient the path goes through a conspicuous narrowing and then enters a small flat valley with the **Refugi de Fontverd**, 1830m, close to a spring. Go past the hut on the right side and then the path ascends through a wood again and in the slowly broadening valley comes back to the same level almost as the stream. After a cattle gate go past a hut on the right of the path which lies in a delightful valley plain with branching side streams. Take no notice of the following turn-off right over logs across the stream to the Maiana pass and into the Perafita valley and continue along the left hand side of the Riu Madriu. Your attention is drawn to the steep granite faces of the Serra del Sirvent. The path moves away from the stream temporarily and gets steeper, then once more moves closer to the stream.

Pass a cattle gate and walk onto the pretty Pla de l'Ingla, an elongated meadow which provides a cattle pasture in summer. On the other side of the stream on the hill there's a shepherd's hut and logs laid across the water lead over to it. However stay on the valley path and walk to the end of the pastureland where the **Refugi Riu dels Orris**, 2230m, is already visible. Ascend just a little further to reach the mountain hut.

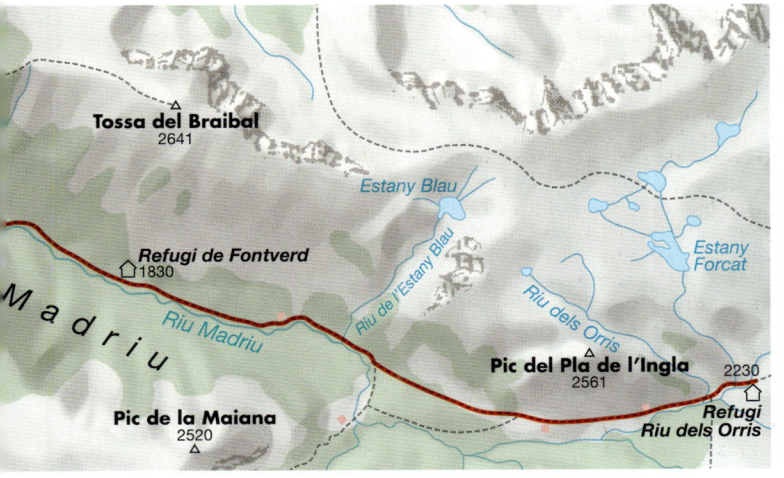

Parc Natural Cadí – Moixeró and upper Cerdanya

The national park southeast of Andorra extends across a length of 30km parallel to the central ridge of the Pyrenees. Geologically of younger origin, the limestone massif forms an almost uninterrupted mountain barrier with a striking contrast between the moderately inclined slopes in the south and the sheer north-facing cliffs whose vertical rock faces reach heights of up to 500m. The extensive woodland and green mountain meadows at the foot of the limestone towers provide the most beautiful contrast.

The imposing north precipices are marked by steep, deep-cut valleys which give the mountain range its distinct structure. Some of these channels make the direct approach onto the sub alpine slopes of the mountain ridge technically more or less difficult. The ridge 'peaks' line up along the northern edge one after another with barely distinguishable height variations. If you approach from the south all you will see is an insignificant chain of hills. But the moment you are standing at the edge of the spectacular cliffs you are rewarded with a view of the rock bastions which are as dramatic as they are interesting.

An ascent from the north affects the same kind of surprise after you have negotiated the stony steep slopes when, beyond the pass, the broadly sweeping grassy high plain unexpectedly stretches out ahead inviting you to wander at will and enjoy the views.

Village springs in Tuixén.

The Ruta dels Segadors had a folklore even before Picasso used it to make the crossing of the Sierra de Cadí in 1906 after a summer stay in Gósol. The comfortable traverse over the Pas dels Gosolans is named after the itinerant workers from Gósol who set off in early summer to look for work in the fields and farmsteads around Bellver de Cerdanya. According to tradition they played music on the pass to let the inhabitants of Bellver know of their arrival. The well-maintained Ruta dels Segadors links in a day's walk the agriculturally poor sunny side of the Sierra de Cadí with the fertile valley of the Río Segre.

The eastern side of the national park includes the Sierra de Moixeró, with clearly lower altitudes, which is separated by the Tancalaporta pass. The Fenyes Altes de Moixeró, with their 2260m form, the highest mass with a densely wooded and moderately steep north side and a sheer southern face. The mountain region around Tosa d'Alp is characterised by the ski complexes of Masella and La Molina which unfortunately spoil the visual impact of the landscape.

Pedraforca, a name and a distinctive mountain shape, is one of the most beautiful mountains on the Iberian peninsula. It consists of two massif mountain domes separated by a broad and steeply sloping scree gully. Coming from the east in the direction of Saldes you have the 'stone fork', literally translated, in sight. The massif is separated by the intensively wooded Gresolet valley of the Cadí mountains and particularly on its northern face has some magnificently formed walls which contain high grade challenges for mountaineers and climbers.

Even if you prefer to be on foot, you ought to consider a drive along the B-400 at the edge of the national park. Together with excellent mountain views you will be delighted by the still largely unspoiled villages like Josa de Cadí, Gósol or Tuixén.

The valley basin of the Riu Segre reaching as far as Puigcerdà runs north of the national park. From the tectonic U-shaped valley which was filled up by a lake in geological times, rises the central ridge of the Pyrenees and peaks in the border mountains with France at heights of around 2900m. You can find high alpine scenery here and there, more especially around Pic de Calm Colomer, but the extensively moderate mountain slopes are more predominant, for example, the centrally situated Puigpedrós which is a popular objective for a walk due to its fantastic views.

Vall de la Llosa running from north to south is the longest and at the same time most beautiful mountain valley in the area. It used to be a significant link between Andorra with France, and thanks to the development and extension of roads and tracks, you are easily able to explore the area as far as its upper course.

37 Vall de la Llosa

Expedition through one of the most beautiful of the Cerdanya valleys

Cal Jan de la Llosa – Prado Xuixirà – Cabana dels Esparvers and back

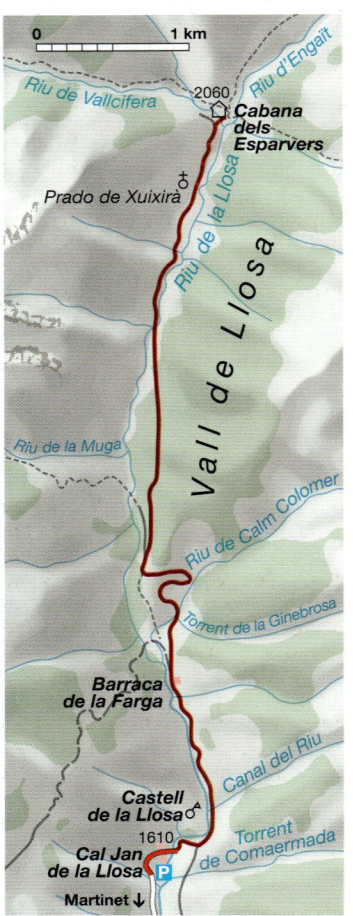

Location: Martinet, 1000m.
Starting point: Cal Jan de la Llosa, 1610m. From Martinet at first to Lles de Cerdanya and then on to Viliella; from there along a track about 2.5km long as far as Cal Jan. Park at the barrier just before the farmstead.
Walking times: Cal Jan de la Llosa – Prado Xuixirà 1¾ hrs.; Prado Xuixirà – Cabana dels Esparvers ½ hr.; return 1¾ hrs.; total time 4 hrs.
Height difference: 450m.
Grade: easy valley walk along roadways and hiking paths; GR 11-10/107.
Refreshments: no opportunities along the way; Lles de Cerdanya; Martinet.
Tip: the track is drivable up to a point. With Viliella as the starting point for your walk, add another hour in total to your walking time.
The Cabana dels Esparvers is a tiny self-catering hut with 6 places.

The valley of the Riu de la Llosa has attracted a lot of attention for a long time. Local legends had dreadful monsters living there. For the inhabitants of the village it was an important link to Andorra and into the French Foix and Querol valleys and it was threatened recently by a project to build a reservoir and tunnel. For the time being a delightful valley remains which offers extensively unspoiled countryside.

Walk along the roadway to the **Cal Jan de la Llosa**, past the fort-like farmstead and immediately afterwards across the wooden bridge over the Riu de la Llosa. After a few

Cabana dels Esparvers.

minutes you meet a roadway coming up from the right which you follow to the left.
A few steps further on you come to a barrier and the path gradually ascends up the valley. You can see the remains of the Castell de la Llosa on the other side of the stream on a granite hill. Just after a cattle gate you pass the derelict Barraca de la Farga, then you walk through a pretty widening of the valley. At the end of the valley the path starts ascending some bends in the course of which you cross the tributaries of the Riu de Calm Colomer several times. At a fork stay on the main path which soon runs on the level. After a second cattle gate cross over to the other side of the stream on a wooden bridge. The valley broadens out again then there's a short incline and you reach the idyllic **Prado de Xuixirà**, 2011m, where the roadway ends. Walk through the beautiful pastureland where there's a place of worship and a broken down forest hut and follow the clear footpath which ascends quickly above the valley and comes to the Riu de Vallcivera flowing in from the left. Here, on a wobbly bridge of logs, change over to the other side of the stream where you go uphill a little way to arrive at the **Cabana dels Esparvers**, 2060m, lying in its picturesque location.

38 Puigpedrós, 2914m

Extremely comfortable ascent to the summit of Cerdanya with superb views

Refugi de Malniu – Coll de les Mulleres – Puigpedrós and back

Location: Meranges, 1530m.
Starting point: Refugi de Malniu, 2138m. Access along a track from Meranges for which you have to pay a toll. After the village follow the signs for Als Llacs. All the subsequent junctions along the track are signposted. Big car park at the hut at the end of the track.
Walking times: Refugi de Malniu – Coll de les Mulleres 1¼ hrs.; Coll de les Mulleres – Puigpedrós 1¼ hrs.; return 2 hrs.; total time 4 ½ hrs.
Height difference: 776m.
Grade: easy walk with some steep sections. At first a short way on the GR11, then the path is marked with cairns.
Refreshments: Refugi de Malniu; Meranges.

The normal ascent onto the just under 3000m high Puigpedrós is too easy for many mountain walkers who prefer more challenging alternatives like the climb through the Circ d'Engorgs to the west of the peak. However, here you can enjoy the usual and more leisurely route where there's plenty to see and explore with views from the summit in all directions.

At the **Refugi** follow the signpost for Puigpedrós (Recomentat). For a short way the route is identical to the GR11 to the Portella d'Engorgs. It takes you over the stream which runs from Estany Sec and afterwards through beautiful sloping pastures gradually uphill to the junction. The GR continues straight ahead, but you leave it here and take the path turning off right. It ascends the hillside cut through by rivulets, levels out later on and comes to a conspicuous furrow in the slope where it appears to continue on the other side on the eroded slope covered in small stones. However, stay on this side of the furrow and go uphill to the right following the cairns. They lead more or less directly and sometimes up a steep gradient to the **Coll de les Mulleres**, 2497m. Puigpedrós can be seen clearly in the north.

Now go to the right and at first following the line of the col to the northeast, walk past a sedimented

pool and then ascend a 'grass corridor' before the path swings abruptly northwards.

A steep incline right across the slope brings you to the long-drawn-out and broad ridge of Puigpedrós which from here, doesn't seem to have a particularly distinct shape. Take any route across the gentle foothills and head towards the summit dome which is formed from slabs of granite all piled up on top of one another. For the last few metres to the top there are two possibilities: either scramble over the piles of rocks in a direct line or keep to the base of the summit on the right and reach **Puigpedrós**, 2914m, ascending over easier ground from the back. Either way, a superb mountain view is assured.

Cn Puigpedrós – view across to the Sierra de Cadí.

39 Estanys de Malniu, 2310m

Pleasant promenade beside the lake at Meranges

Refugi de Malniu – Estanys de Malniu and back

At the start of the walk – Refugi de Malniu.

Location: Meranges, 1530m.
Starting point: Refugi de Malniu, 2138m (for access see Walk 38).
Walking times: Refugi de Malniu – Estanys de Malniu 1¼ hrs.; return 1 hr.; total time 2¼ hrs.
Height difference: 172m.
Grade: stroll along marked hiking path.
Refreshments: Refugi de Malniu; Meranges.

The ground around the small Malniu lakes is an enchanting spot. Pretty lake shores, forests, sloping meadows with babbling streams and the beautiful view of the mountain scenery invite you to while away some time. In summer and at weekends there's lots of bustling activity here, particularly since barbecue and picnic sites have been constructed at the refuge.
From the **Refugi** cross over the Rec de Malniu and immediately after the ridge take the hiking park left marked white and yellow. It keeps on the

right of the stream and leads up a gentle incline through the pretty landscape of granite rock, carpets of grass and pine forest. As it gets flatter it reaches the southern tip of the first **Estany de Malniu**, 2270m. Stay on the path on the right hand shore as far as the northern end of the lake, leave the path there to the right and ascend across the almost barren slope for a few metres to the second and smaller lake, **Estany de Malniu**, 2310m. This sedimented lake presents a charming sight with its islands of flowers and water veins. The surrounding grassy hillsides, gigantic granite boulders and the view over to the Sierra de Cadí complete the beautiful landscape.

Rocks like art sculptures.

40 Circular walk at the foot of the Sierra de Cadí

Picturesque villages, a Romanesque chapel and great views of the Cadí rock faces

Cava – el Boscal – Ansovell – Cava

Location: Arsèguel, 920m.
Starting point: Cava, 1286m. Car park at the entrance to the village. From Arsèguel go along the signposted valley road to Cava.
Walking times: Cava – el Boscal 1¾ hrs.; el Boscal – Ansovell ½ hr.; Ansovell – Cava 1 hr.; total time 3¼ hrs.
Height difference: about 430m.
Grade: easy walk on forest paths, GR150 from el Boscal.
Refreshments: no opportunities along the way; El Pont de Arsèguel.

This peaceful circular walk roams through valleys full of forests and links two characteristic mountain villages with prettily restored houses and at the chapel of Mare de Déu de Boscal reaches a fantastic viewing point of the steeply towering rock bastions of the Cadí mountains.

The circular path begins at the entrance to the village of **Cava** along the roadway which goes downhill left and is signposted for Corta del Roig. After a well on the left of the path cross over a little stream and afterwards go past a sign for the Parc Natural. The path gently descends through a light oak wood to the Riu de Cadí. Go across the bridge over the stream and then the roadway goes up an easy incline along beside the densely wooded Puig Rodon and comes to a grassy small col where an inconspicuous level path goes off right in a westerly direction as the roadway continues downhill

The pretty little village of Cava with the Sierra de Cadí as a backdrop.

again. Turn right onto the new path which becomes more obvious again after a few steps and now walk through the dense pine forest. The path crosses side streams and widens out into an old roadway which slowly ascends onto a gentle col. This is where you reach the pastureland of **el Boscal**, 1469m, with the large chapel of the same name at the edge of the path. Take the GR150 past the chapel and after a few minutes you walk onto a wide grassy slope coming down from the small elevation of Turó de Boscal which gives you a fantastic view of the Sierra de Cadí cut through with steep channels, as well as the upper sweeps of the Cerdanya mountains in the north. The GR leads down to **Ansovell**, 1338m, goes on the right past the church and a few steps straight ahead along the slightly descending village path to the white and red waymarkers. Leave the village path here on the right and follow an at first inconspicuous grassy track which then becomes more obvious. It leads through the forest where the sometimes hardly visible sections of path are compensated by frequent waymarkers. Descend the valley hillside of the Riu de Cadí and at an old stone bridge you come back to the stream where you ascend on the other side steeply uphill to **Cava**.

41 Prat de Cadí, 1820m

Green high plateau in front of a superb rock bastion

Estana – Prat de Cadí and back

Location: Martinet, 1000m.
Starting point: Estana, 1500m. Car park at the entrance to the village which is reached from Martinet via Villec along the signposted road.
Walking times: Estana – Prat de Cadí 1¼ hrs.; return 1 hr.; total time 2¼ hrs.
Height difference: 320m.
Grade: easy walk along a yellow and white marked path.
Refreshments: no opportunities along the way; Estana (restaurant) and Martinet.

This is one of the most beautiful places on the north side of the Sierra de Cadí. The Prat de Cadí lies like a green carpet at the foot of the 500m towering rock face whose striking buttresses and steep grooves present a dramatic sight – especially in the evening light.

Go through **Estana** on the road and at the eastern end of the village continue along the adjoining roadway. Past a small barbecue and picnic area you arrive in 10 minutes at the Coll de Pallers where the nature park of Cadí-Moixeró begins. At first continue straight ahead along the leisurely ascending roadway and soon turn off right onto the signposted hiking path and then through a fairytale wood. The route temporarily becomes a little unclear across an eroded slope with a striking red colour, but then continues more distinctly again as it goes uphill to the Collet Roig with a trig point. Over the small col you change back into the Bastanist valley again from the Quer valley. The now practically level path runs through Austrian pines and fir trees, crosses a stream and shortly afterwards joins with a roadway ascending from the left. Go a few steps more along this roadway until you reach the **Prat de Cadí**, 1820m, in front of an impressive mountain backdrop. A refreshing spring (Fuente del Pi) is to be found on the other side of the circular meadow and a little to the left.

At your destination – Prat de Cadí.

42 Refugi Prat d'Aguiló (Cèsar August Torras), 2037m

Walking along the Ruta dels Segadors, a path rich in tradition

Nas – Cortal de l'Oriol – Coll de l'Home Mort – Refugi Prat d'Aguiló and back

Location: Bellver de Cerdanya, 1020m.
Starting point: Nas, 1225m. From Bellver de Cerdanya along the signposted road to Nas.
Walking times: Nas – Cortal de l'Oriol 1¼ hrs.; Cortal de l'Oriol – Coll de l'Home Mort 1¼ hrs.; Coll de l'Home Mort – Refugi Prat d'Aguiló ½ hr.; return 2½ hrs.; total time 5½ hrs.
Height difference: 815m.
Grade: long walk on roadways and hiking paths with varying degrees of steepness; white and yellow waymarkers.
Refreshments: Refugi Prat d'Aguiló; Bellver de Cerdanya.
Linking tip: Comabona (see Walk 43).
Tip: you can also begin the walk at the Cortal de l'Oriol (a drivable track to that point) which is a good place to start if you want to make the ascent to Comabona as well (Walk 43).

This walk goes along the path that was used formerly by the reapers from Gósol in the southern foothills of the Sierra de Cadí. Every year around the start of June the agricultural workers used to cross the mountain to look for work in the pastures and fields around Bellver. Follow their tracks through the valley of Ridolaina up to the mountain hut at the edge of gently sloping meadows (Prat d'Aguiló) where the Sierra de Cadí is displayed in panoramic format. The refuge is the starting point for the ascent up to Comabona, the most popular peak in the Sierra.

In **Nas** keep to the white and yellow waymarkers that lead to the roadway at the exit to the village. It runs through enclosed meadows to the signposted natural park boundary where you take a shortcut to the right and after a quarter of an hour rejoin the roadway. At a small protrusion a few steps further on you have a lovely view into the Ridolaina valley with Comabona attracting your attention. Walk along the roadway up the valley to a narrow left hand bend where a waymarker on a tree indicates another shortcut. Ascending steeply up through a wood you meet the roadway again at a spring (Font Tosca) which you follow to a fork with a second spring (Font de l'Orri). At this point you

Ridolaina valley.

have reached **Cortal de l'Oriol**, 1520m. The left hand turn-off leads to the nearby shepherd's hut, but you stay on the right and slightly downhill you then pass a barrier and come to a landslide area with a sign indicating the danger of rock fall: as you cross the slope be sure to take care and not to knock down any rocks!

Cross over two streams. A little further on the path leaves the roadway to the left and after a few metres meets an old little roadway which immediately begins to ascend. Follow this to the left and then it becomes a forest path where you go steeply uphill and meet another roadway. This now ascends some sharp bends up to a metal bivouac after which it continues leisurely over to the track that comes up from Montellá. Following the track you arrive at the **Coll de l'Home Mort**, 1850m.

Continue left here and after just under 10 minutes take the path leading off to the left on a narrow right hand bend. A waymarker on a tree indicates the start of the path. Ascending through the lightly wooded slope you come back to the track. Follow this to the car park and barrier. The lovely hillsides beyond extend around the hut. A few minutes later you have arrived at the **Refugi Prat d'Aguiló**, 2037m.

43 Comabona, 2547m

Classic summit walk in the Sierra de Cadí

Refugi Prat d'Aguiló – Pas dels Gosolans – Comabona and back

Location: Martinet, 1000m.
Starting point: Ref. Prat d'Aguiló, 2037m. From Martinet in the direction of Montellá, but take the signposted track beforehand to the car park just before the refuge.
Walking times: Refugi Prat d'Aguiló – Pas dels Gosolans 1¼ hrs.; Pas dels Gosolans – Comabona ½ hr.; return 1½ hrs.; total time 3¼ hrs.
Height difference: 510m.
Grade: moderately difficult ascent with steep gradient, but no problems technically in normal conditions. White and red waymarkers to the Pas dels Gosolans, at times also GR waymarkers.
Refreshments: Ref. Prat d'Aguiló; Martinet.
Linking tip: with Walk 42 (Refugi Prat d'Aguiló).
Tip: the good 12 km long track is unfortunately in a bad state of repair, but is passable with care. Alternative access on the Ruta dels Segadors with a stay overnight in the refuge if necessary (see Walk 42).

Refugi Prat d'Aguiló.

You won't be surprised to know that Comabona is the most walked summit in the Sierra de Cadí and is easily identified by its elongated range of mountains. The relative carefreeness of the ascent and the beauty of the rock formations which can be seen from different perspectives along the way, combine to make an extremely attractive programme. On top of that comes the surprising contrast in the landscape between the sheer north face of the Sierra and its softly rising mountain ridges on which you can enjoy a walk in all directions. A brilliant walk!

After the **Refugi Prat d'Aguiló** take the furrowed path in a southerly di-

Fas dels Gosolans – surprisingly even slope of the Sierra.

rection and go up across grassy slopes. Continue past a spring with a hollowed out tree trunk, then round a few sharp bends to a grassy ledge with a light stand of pine trees. The path soon leads onto stony and open ground and winds its way uphill below the striking Roca d'Aguiló. Then in a southwesterly direction cross over to a small protrusion with beautiful views. From here the path winds directly uphill and continues up across a hillside. After a steep incline up the slope of the col you are standing on the **Pas dels Gosolans**, 2410m, where you have reached the back of the Sierra de Cadí. The direct route to Comabona continues away from the edge of the mountain crags and descends diagonally to the left into the small valley basin with the Font Tordera. Past the spring and through characteristically karst terrain keep heading for an inconspicuous pre-summit of Comabona and from this go over to **Comabona**, 2547m, recognised by its small summit pillar. Magnificent views in all directions – amongst those, the Pyrenees central ridge in the north and the Pedraforca massif in the south clearly separated from the Sierra de Cadí.

44 Penyes Altes de Moixeró, 2276m

The most beautiful peak in the eastern part of the Parc Natural del Cadí-Moixeró

Piste zum Coll de Pendís – Coll de Dental – Penyes Altes de Moixeró and back

Location: Riu de Cerdanya, 1160m.
Starting point: track to the Coll de Pendís, 1780m. In Riu de Cerdanya orientate yourself towards the main square with its town hall and church. Continue from there along the road going off opposite the town hall which becomes a track. Partly asphalted and fairly drivable it leads past the Refugi del Serrat de les Esposes II and divides after about 12km. Park your car before the barrier. (Right goes to the Refugi de l'Ingla, straight on to the Coll de Pendís).
Walking times: car park – Coll de Dental 1¼ hrs.; Coll de Dental – Penyes Altes de Moixeró 1¼ hrs.; return 2¼ hrs.; total time 4¾ hrs.
Height difference: 496m.
Grade: walk along roadways and hiking paths; predominantly moderate inclines, a bit steeper on the last section to the summit. GR150 -1 from the Coll de Dental.
Refreshments: no opportunities along the way; Refugi del Serrat de les Esposes II; Bellver de Cerdanya.
Alternative: return from the Coll de Dental via **Turó de Prat Agre**, 2012m. At the Coll de Dental take the ascending GR continuing from the col. It ascends the long ridge of Turó and stays for a while on the ridge, often over rough ground, but well indicated by abundant GR waymarkings and cairns. The path descends quickly and joins the track to the Coll de Pendís. Go along this to the right to return to your starting point. From the Coll de Dental about 1 hr.

While moderate southern slopes and vertical northern precipices characterise the Sierra de Cadí, quite the reverse is true of the eastern Moixeró mountains. On the summit of Penyes Altes to the south you are standing above a sheer drop. From here you can enjoy the wide view across the valley of Llobregat and over to Comabona and Pedraforca.
At the **car park** take the roadway ascending left immediately after the bar-

Coll de Dental.

rier. After just under a quarter of an hour it meets another roadway which comes up from the Coll de Trapa. Continue right uphill and after a barrier the roadway levels out and you come through a shady pine wood with rhododendrons. Then there's a grassy platform on the slope from where you go quickly up an incline to the Pla de Moixeró, a treeless col. Now leave the roadway on your left hand side (it leads down some tracks to pastureland with a water reservoir and a shepherd's hut) and take one of the cross paths which run at the same level across the slopes on the right over to the **Coll de Dental**, 1985m.

From here your path is waymarked in white and red. It heads eastwards across the grassy hillsides of Moixeró and stays at the same level, then turns right and slowly ascends through a light stand of pines to the Coll de Moixeró. From there proceed through a wood and a little later on you reach a small clearing with a signpost to the Penyes Altes. Ascending through the wood you now start the summit climb, following, as you do so, the clear GR waymarkers. The path goes at first on the right of the ridge, then after a while changes over to the left hand side to go round a rocky knoll, then swings sharply to the right onto the ridge and follows this to the summit of **Penyes Altes de Moixeró**, 2276m.

45 Vulturó, 2638m

Onto the roof of the Sierra de Cadí

Collada de Jovell – l'Osca – Vulturó and back

Bizarre rock structures in the Sierra de Cadí.

Location: Josa, 1431m.
Starting point: Collada de Jovell, 1790m. At Josa a signposted and good drivable track branches off from the road along which you come to a grassy col after about 6km.
Access is also possible along the track from Cornellana, in this case about 8km.
Walking times: Collada de Jovell – l'Osca 1¾ hrs.; l'Osca – Vulturó 1¼ hrs.; return 2½ hrs.; total time 5½ hrs.
Height difference: 848m.
Grade: summit walk with hardly any paths over really steep karst terrain as far as l'Osca, from there moderate gradients. Although it's supposed to be the GR150 -1, there's neither a clear path nor obvious waymarkers present. However, the ascent has no problems of orientation and poses hardly any difficulties for experienced mountain walkers. Dangerous in fog. Be careful of rapid changes in the weather and developing thunderstorms!
Refreshments: no opportunities on the way; Josa.
Tip: the southern ascent is without shade, so set off in good time in summer and take plenty of fluids with you.

If you are acquainted with the northern slopes of the Sierra de Cadí, on the ascent of the southern slope you will become acquainted with an exciting and impressive contrast in the landscape of this mountain. The bizarre rock formations of protrusions and gullies along the steep precipices offer a some dramatic scenery and the panoramic views from the highest point in the Sierra de Cadí do credit to Vulturó from where in the west you can see a

considerable number of peaks in the central Pyrenees like Cotiella and Maladeta, while to the south, you can look over large parts of Catalonia with the coastal mountains of the Costa Brava as far as Montserrat in front of Barcelona.

There's a sign for the **Collada de Jovell** and you take this as your starting point. The southern slope lying ahead is dominated by box trees and low bushes and you have a good view of it from here. Numerous narrow eroded grooves and slabs of loose and solid eroded rock open up the slope and offer plenty of opportunities to find a way through. As you continue along the col's axis start up the slope and always keep going north on your ascent as you avoid several large areas of scree in the middle of the slope and climb up on their right hand side. Looking back you can see the Collada de Jovell from every point of the ascent until you step over a rim after about 550 vertical metres and come to some less steep ground with meadows, called **l'Osca**, 2450m.

From here the sweeping rise of the Sierra de Cadí emerges and you now head across this in a northeasterly direction towards the edge of the slopes. You might even come across the odd painted waymarker or cairn, but the latter is more likely to be an accident of nature. With a pleasant gradient you reach the edge of the sheer rock faces of the mountains and walk along the impressive crags eastwards and up to Puig de les Gralleres. Vulturó lies opposite, separated by a cleft, the Canal Baridana de Josa. Descend to the col and then go uphill again along the steep mountain ridge. A small protrusion just before the summit is easily overcome after which you quickly reach **Vulturó**, 2638m.

46 Pedraforca, 2497m

A landmark of Catalonian tourism

Refugi Lluís Estasen – Coll del Verdet – Pollegó superior and back

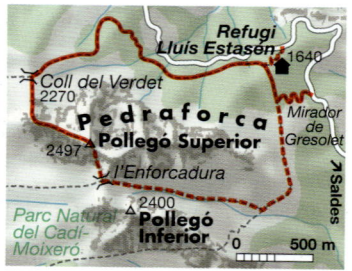

Location: Saldes, 1120m.
Starting point: Refugi Lluís Estasen, 1640m.

Just after Saldes (in the direction of Gósol) go along the signposted road to the Mirador de Gresolet. Either park here or continue along the road and about 800m on the adjoining track to a little house. Both places have signs indicating the way to the hut.

Walking times: Refugi Lluís Estasen – Coll del Verdet 2¼ hrs.; Coll del Verdet – Pollegó superior 1 hr.; return 2½ hrs.; total time 5¾ hrs.

Height difference: 857m.

Grade: predominantly strenuous ascent, with some very steep inclines and sections of climbing in the summit area (I/II) which all make for a demanding walk. There are white and yellow waymarkers to the Coll del Verdet and the climbing routes are indicated with yellow signs. Be careful of rapid weather changes and developing thunderstorms.

Refreshments: Refugi Lluís Estasen; Saldes.

Alternative: descent via the Canal de la Tartera. The broad band of scree which drops down from the col between the twin peaks, provides you with an opportunity to make a circular walk. From Pollegó superior a steep path descends to the col, the so-called 'Enforcadura'. From here continue down through the steep scree-filled, partly broken gully. At the end of the Tartera go through the wood on the left back to the refuge. Time from Pollegó superior: 2 hrs.

For many mountain lovers Pedraforca is the perfect example of a mountain and therefore a popular summit to aim for. The massif derives its name 'fork of stone' from the unmistakable shape it presents from its eastern side: two sheer peaks which are separated by a deep notch. The ascent from the Refugi Lluís Estasen runs along the imposing north side and shows the diverse beauty of the massif.

At the **Refugi** follow the signpost to Pedraforca pel Coll del Verdet. The path through the wood stays at first more or less on the level, crosses the boulder-strewn Canal del Riambau and then clearly forces you to go uphill. At a fork in a path turn off left following the path with a wooden sign to El verdet, while straight ahead goes on to Set Fonts. There's a beautiful view on the really steep path of the vertical rock faces of the northern slope where you frequently see climbers. The path levels out temporarily and runs along a shelf with a wonderful view of the lower areas of rock and the walls with their various colours. It brings you to a conspicuous gully where the path ascends on the left hand side, then goes across a pine-covered slope with exposed tree roots serving as steps. Leaving the trees behind you, start up the slope of the Coll del Verdet and the dirt path keeps to the right and skirts the base of a rock wall – do not be tempted to stray from the well-trodden and scree-covered tracks in the middle of the slope. You arrive at the small **Coll del Verdet**, 2270m, ideal as a stopping point before the summit section.

Following the ridge of the col go at first on the left, then on the right hand side directly towards a rocky slope where a large blue P marks the approach to the first climbing section. Keep to the yellow, but now rather faded route waymarkings as you make the enjoyable climb up the rock which has good friction. They lead up to a platform with a full view of the summit section. Continue uphill following the line of the ridge. At first more on the level, then with a bit of descent and ascent again, you come to the base of the steep dome-shaped summit of rock. A last section of climbing up the broad base – find your way again by the yellow waymarkers – and you are standing on the highest point of Pedraforca, **Pollegó superior**, 2497m.

Last section to the summit.

Vall de Núria

The mountain ranges around Vall de Nuria in the province of Ripolles form the last large structures of the central Pyrenean ridge. The hills to the east gradually descend onto lower mountain ranges and in the Alberas they have a typically Mediterranean character. The highest peak is Puigmal at 2913m in the west of the valley. A long series of peaks stretches from Puigmal to the north and in a arc to the east along the border with France with little variation in height around the 2900m mark. One mountain chain extending from Pic de Fossa del Gargant to the south separates Vall de Nuria from Coma de Freser, the upper valley of the Riu de Freser which leaves the group around Pic de l'infern. Between the hardly defined different peaks of the border ridge there are some flat and accessible passes which provide lovely crest walks and circular walks between the side-valleys. Amongst the principal types of rock, slate is prevalent in the dome-shaped mountains and soft valleys of the main ridge; in zones of extreme erosion where all grass cover has disappeared, the rock sometimes leaves behind a scree-like impression. Formations of gneiss have evolved that have sheered off abruptly like the Roques de Totlomon or the deep gorge of the Riu de Nuria. Metamorphic limestone rock also contributes to the phenomena of karst and of hollows in the rock.

At just under 2000m at the intersection of the side-valleys lies the Santuari de Núria, a legendary pilgrim site of Catalanists. They pay homage here to the Virgen de Núria, protector of Pyrenean shepherds. According to legend, Sant Gil laid the foundation stone for a hermitage in the year 700 in a cave, the impetus for the later building of the first chapel which was first documented in the 12th century and constantly altered and extended over the centuries. Núria is dominated today by an enormous complex of buildings in which there can be found a hotel, restaurants, shops, exhibition rooms and a large information centre.

A cog railway, the Cremallera, runs from Ribes de Freser via Queralbs up to Santuari along a bold stretch of track across the gorge walls of the Riu de Núria. A big attraction in itself, it makes a good 700 vertical metres of walking up into the Núria circle of mountains considerably easier. The big peaks which would present challenging mountain walks, can be seen in close proximity. However, you should not miss the opportunity to make the ascent and descent along the fantastic mountain trail through the Gorgues de Núria, part of the classic GR11. Getting a closer view of the cascading waterfalls and smooth sided rock basins is only possible on foot and even then two huge narrowings in the gorge remain hidden from view and are only accessible to experienced canyoning enthusiasts.

Cog railway on its way through Vall de Núria.

47 Puigmal, 2913m

Circular walk over the highest 'peak' of the Núria valley

Núria – Coll de Finestrelles – Pic del Segre – Puigmal – Núria

Location: Queralbs, 1236m.
Starting point: Santuari de Núria, 1967m. Accessible either on the Cremallera or along the Camí Vell through Núria valley (see Walk 48).
Walking times: Núria – Coll de Finestrelles 1¾ hrs.; Coll de Finestrelles – Pic del Segre ¾ hr.; Pic del Segre – Puigmal ¾ hr.; Puigmal – Núria 2 hrs.; total time 5¼ hrs.
Height difference: 1050m with ascents and descents.
Grade: long circular walk with a big variation in height and some steep inclines.
Blue marked path as far as the Coll de Finestrelles; from there a ridge path waymarked with cairns to Puigmal. Obvious return path to Núria.
Refreshments: Núria; Queralbs.
Tip: see p. 13 for the Cremallera timetable.

Puigmal – not especially striking summit.

L'Embut – underground outflow of the valley stream.

Puigmal – a mountain of contrasts. Sometimes called jokingly 'coma de vaca' (hill of the cow) you are greeted by an array of fluttering flags on the summit. Puigmal is not particularly attractive to look at, but as Núria's highest mountain it obviously enjoys much respect. It is, perhaps, also the far-reaching panoramic views which attract many to its summit. However, this circular walk offers more than that – it gives you a good general impression of the mountains and valleys in the western part of Vall de Núria.

The path begins after the large **Núria** building complex at the signpost for Puigmal / Finistrelles. From here follow the track running parallel to a ski tow at the end of which you change over to the other side of the Torrent de Finstrelles on a concrete bridge. Go left up the slope for a few metres to a second similar signpost by a covered water control point where you follow the well-trodden path ascending diagonally left up the hillside. Right after crossing the Torrent de la Coma de l'Embut flowing in from the left you come to a fork (this is the point where you meet the path again on the return); keep straight ahead and continue uphill by the side of the left hand side stream in the Y valley lying straight ahead. After a steep incline cross over the stream and walk away from it to climb round the rock protrusions of the Roc de la Maula on the right. The path zigzags up to a midway col after which there's a small waterfall. From here onwards the Coll de Finistrelles is easily visible. The path now runs diagonally right across the hillside and arrives at the stream. Cross over it and also a second little stream a bit further up, and then continue up round the long, in places elongated bends gradually up the slope of the col to the **Coll de Finistrelles**, 2604m, with a cross.

Now continue left up along the mountain ridge, at first on the eastern side, then directly on the broad ridge and in-between the 'double peak'. The path heads towards the grassy summit slope and reaches **Pic de Segre**, 2843m. Descend a scree path to a midway pass, then steeply uphill on the southeastern flank until you reach the crest of the ridge again. Follow it for a while then the path goes round an elevation on the right and leads over to the Collada d'Er, 2760m. From here the ascent begins to Puigmal partly

Núria – today a modern tourist centre.

on obvious paths, partly over slabs and stones. At first you keep more to the left of the summit ridge, but in-between times walk directly on the crest and eventually the path swings onto the right hand side of the ridge and quickly comes to the unmistakable 'summit' of **Puigmal**, 2913m.

The return sets off from the summit in a northeasterly direction (the path heading south descends to the Collada de Fontalba!) and leads down some scree-covered zigzag bends on the mountain slopes into the broad valley. In the valley bottom follow the Torrent de la Coma de l'Embut, cross over it and keep on the right hand side as you continue down the valley. After a small waterfall the stream suddenly disappears in a cave; if you walk back about 50m along the dry streambed that the path crosses a little later, you can see the natural spectacle close-by. Continuing along the left hand side of the stream you then meet a fork in the path where a path on the right changes over onto the other side again and descends across the Pla de l'Ortigar to Núria. The path keeps straight ahead at first above the cleft of a short gorge and then descends the steep grassy slope quickly down to the stream which is now running with water again. Walk along its left hand bank towards the valley of the Torrent de Finistrelles where you meet the ascent path. Turn right here to return to **Núria**.

48 Along the Camí Vell from Queralbs to Núria

The old path through Núria gorge

Queralbs – Pont de Cremal – Núria

Cua de Cavall waterfall (horse's tail).

Location: Queralbs, 1236m.
Starting point: Queralbs, 1236m. Car parks at the entrance to the village.
Walking times: Queralbs – Pont de Cremal 1¼ hrs.; Pont de Cremal – Núria 1¾ hrs.; total time 3 hrs.
Height difference: 731m.
Grade: ascent up through the valley with some really steep sections. GR11.
Refreshments: Núria; Queralbs.
Tip: see page 13 for the Cremallera timetable.

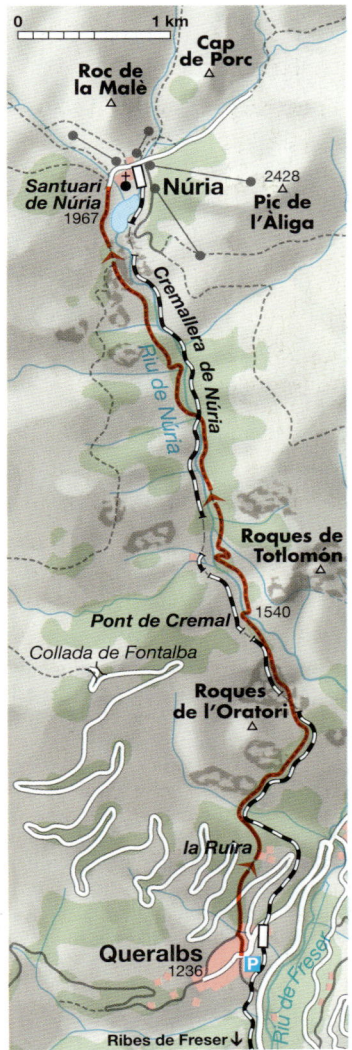

The old path through the deep valley of Riu de Núria was, before the start of work on the cog railway, the direct approach to the place of pilgrimage in its high location. Today the well constructed path offers a fascinating opportunity to get a closer look at the impressive and varied gorge landscape and its fabulous surroundings of rocks.

At the entrance to the village of **Queralbs** there's a sign indicating the start of the Camí de Núria. It leaves the village to the right and further up crosses the track leading to the Collada de Fontalba. Past the last houses it runs across sloping meadows and comes to the walled Font de la Ruira on the left of the path. For a short while it runs closely above the cog railway across densely overgrown hillsides, at first ascending leisurely, then more rapidly.

The valley of Riu de Freser can be seen opposite which is dominated by the steep crags of Torreneules. Climb over a tunnel of the Cremallera, go past the Refugi Sant Pau, a rock shelter, and walk high above the Riu de Núria towards the

Following the waterfall – canyoning in the Gorgas de Núria.

increasingly narrower valley which ends up in a deep gorge at the exit of which there are beautifully formed cascades and round pools. The Roques de Totlomón tower above.

At the stone **Pont de Cremal**, 1540m, the valley opens out again and you change onto the other side of the more gently flowing stream. The path now gets considerably steeper up the valley hillside above the stream, at first round sharp bends to another rock shelter, the Refugi Sant Rafael, then after a strenuous crossing of the slope it begins to zigzag uphill crossing a covered water channel as it does so. After you have climbed so high above the second gorge of the Riu de Núria, a thundering waterfall, the Salt del Sastre, comes into view. Now alternatively on the level or ascending moderately the path runs up the valley and slowly approaches the stream again and a waterfall called Cua de Cavall, literally meaning 'horse's tail', which alludes to the broad dispersion of the water. As you continue along the path the gradient becomes palpably steeper and you pass several prettily shaped steps and cascades. When the path gets flatter again cross over the stream on a wooden plank underneath the bridge for the cog railway and leisurely ascend the slopes which are covered in gorse, juniper and alpine roses. On the right the Riu de Núria continues to display its beautiful waterfalls and pools. Then the path gets somewhat steeper again and comes to a junction where, if you take the right hand path, you can make a detour to the Mirador de la Creu d'en Riba; from the small rocky hill you can see Núria and the surrounding mountains. Continue straight ahead and past a cross, the Creu d'en Riba, and the path gradually descends and then leads to the **Santuari de Núria**, 1967m. The cog railway will take you back to Queralbs.

There are many deep gorges in Vall de Núria.

49 Through the Gorgues del Freser and along the Camí dels Enginyers

Spectacular walk through valleys and rocky hillsides

Pont de Daió – bridge over the Riu del Freser – Refugi Manelic – Cabana de Pedrisses – Núria

Location: Queralbs, 1236m.
Starting point: Pont de Daió, 1200m. About 1km before Queralbs, immediately after the Alberg-Refugi La Farga, turn off right from the road (sign for Salt del Grill / Coma de Vaca) and drive along the asphalt track as far as the small electricity works; parking before the Daió bridge.
Walking times: Pont de Daió – bridge over the Riu del Freser 1½ hrs.; bridge over the Riu del Freser – Refugi Manelic 1¾ hrs.; Refugi Manelic – Cabana de Pedrisses 2¾ hrs.; Cabana de Pedrisses – Núria 1 hrs.; total time 7 hrs.
Height difference: about 1000m with ascents and descents.

Grade: very long walk demanding good fitness on which there are some very steep ascents to negotiate. Some exposed sections on the Camí dels Enginyers and short scrambles. Generally clear waymarkings, white and green at first as far as the Refugi Manelic, later red waymarkers; the Camí dels Enginyers is part of the GR11.7.
Refreshments: Refugi Manelic in the Pla de Coma de Vaca, 2020m; Queralbs.
Tip: return from Núria to Queralbs with the Cremallera or descend through Vall de Núria (see Walk 48). See page 13 for the Cremallera timetable.
Return from Queralbs to the Pont de Daió ½ hr.

Steep chasms along the Cami dels Enginyers.

The ascent through the valley of Riu de Freser invites you at every step to take a look at the fantastically formed rock faces which dominate the valley in the north. The scenery that you are always invited to admire from a distance – but don't forget the landscape of the valley nearby – can also be experienced at close range on this exciting Camí dels Enginyers in the interior of the mountains and high above the Gorgues del Freser. After an outstanding day's walk you can then take the Cremallera back down to the valley. It's worth mentioning that it's possible to split the walk into two separate ones, each of which is equally impressive.

Cross the **Pont de Daió** to the other side of the Riu del Freser and walk along the shady path close to the stream. Cross over the Torrent del Salt del Grill flowing in from the left on a concrete bridge; then the path climbs steeply up the slope covered in ferns, bushes and small trees, now and then with intermediary flatter areas. As the valley broadens out temporarily and becomes more open, you come onto less precipitous slopes with a more gentle gradient. You are accompanied on the left by some great rock formations dropping down from the Torreneules. As the gradient constantly alternates between being strenuous and then more gentle, you reach the wide and pretty valley plain of la Paradella. The path runs through tall grass with lots of flowers to the end of the broad valley and crosses the Riu del Frese on a **wooden bridge**. A bank of rock up the valley bars your way along the stream which you avoid by going up the slope on the right.

View across to Puigmal.

A section of persistent and strenuous uphill climbing now begins with numerous sharp bends across wooded slopes also covered in flowers which bring you high above the valley stream and afford you the most beautiful views of the rock formations on the other side of the valley. There's a striking contrast between the densely wooded hillside you are walking across and the rugged rock faces opposite divided by grassy slopes and steep gullies. The path then ascends across almost treeless slopes of grass and rock towards a narrowing of the valley further ahead, crosses the slope and eventually becomes noticeably flatter as the Pla de Coma de Vaca (also marked on the map as Planell de les Eugues) comes into view. Several valleys join together on the extensive high plain with pastures and countless side streams. The path now heads towards the valley bottom – on the hillside opposite you can clearly see the start of the Camí dels Enginyers – and makes a short detour through the little side-valley of the Torrent de Bogadé which you now follow on the left or the right hand side to the metal bridge over the Riu del Freser. Go across the bridge to the **Refugi Manelic**, 2020m.

The white and red marked Camí dels Enginyers begins after the hut on the left and below a rain-measuring device. It immediately starts to ascend and runs across the hillside up to the Coll dels Homes. The col is a beautiful viewing point with views of the Gorgues del Freser right across to Puigmal. The path now descends leisurely down the grass covered hillside, sometimes over boulders, and then goes over a rocky ridge. The following path brings you over several more such ridges with some fantastic rock structures. After that the path heads towards a huge cleft with steep rock walls, the Clot de Malinfern, and it seems unimaginable that you can get any further. Turn into the steep gorge and you come to a gully filled with boulders where there is no sign of any tracks (be careful here), but climb about 10m higher over the boulders to the rock face where there are even some waymarkers. You now go up really steeply with some scrambling in places staying close to the rock face where a rope has been fixed to give you support. The path soon becomes freer again and with some more strenuous uphill climbing you reach another small col which is occupied by a bizarre rock figure. Descending again you come to the next col. Afterwards go downhill a bit again and then up to a broader pass. After a few minutes across slopes of grass and flowers go uphill again and the path runs out of a valley with a stream. There's a short bit of scrambling and you continue on the other side of the valley at the same height. The path ascends again just afterwards to a protrusion on the slope and turns once more into a valley where the rocks have now given way to grassy slopes. Cross over a stream and stay for a while on the same level. Past a beautiful rock arch on the left and a little below the path, head towards the conspicuous projecting rock, Castellcervós, beyond which the upper Núria valley comes into view. Continue along the level path to the **Cabana de Pedrisses**, 2140m, which lies a few metres higher up on the slope, then the path swings eventually into Vall de Núria. High above the gorge the path runs along gentle grassy slopes, crosses over the Torrente de Fontnegra and joins a Way of the Cross, the Camí de les Creus. You can either walk along the track down to **Núria** or on the next left hand bend take the shortcut which branches off right.

50 Pic de Noufonts, 2861m

Good views of Núria and the neighbouring French valleys

Núria – Coll de Noucreus – Pic de Noufonts and back

Location: Queralbs, 1236m.
Starting point: Santuari de Núria, 1967m. Accessible either with the Cremallera or along the Camí Vell through the Núria valley (see Walk 48).
Walking: Núria – Coll de Noucreus 2 hrs.; Coll de Noucreus – Pic de Noufonts 1¼ hrs.; return 2¾ hrs.; total time 6 hrs.
Height difference: about 950m with ascents and descents.
Grade: long walk with the pleasantly varied gradients; steep climb only up to Pic de Noufonts. Partly along the GR11, clear path through the Coma de Noucreus as well as on the summit ascent.
Refreshments: Núria; Queralbs.
Tip: see page 13 for the Cremallera timetable.
Alternative: return through the Eina valley. The walk can be made into a circular walk. At Pic de Noufonts at the wrought-iron CEF sign take the descending ridge path in the direction of

Pic d'Eina. It crosses the small col from which the shapeless Pic d'Eina rises up to the north, runs more or less on the level for a way and then descends through scree-covered terrain down to the broad Coll d'Eina with views of the French d'Eyne valley. From the Coll you turn onto the southeastern slope of Puig del Coll d'Eina, following the cairns and blue waymarkers. The path quickly descends the at first scree-covered, then grassy slopes and then some sharp bends bring you down to the stream relatively close to the head of the valley. Cross over the stream and walk along the well-trodden path on the left hand side down the valley as far as the bridge before Núria.

Walking time from Pic de Noufonts to Núria 2¼ hrs.

On Pic de Noufonts.

A circuitous walk with beautiful views, which take you through the valley of the Torrent de Noucreus, ascends up to the pass of the same name which is festooned with crosses and follows the line of the ridge from there which goes with lots of ups-and-downs over to Pic de Noufonts in the centre of the circle of mountains of Núria. The summit offers a superb view of the dramatic mountain ranges of the French Valleta valley.

In **Núria** go from the station of the Cremallera to the valley station of the Telecabina, follow the track on the left and go past a chair lift to the meteorological station. Afterwards you come to an little old stone bridge with a signpost which points straight ahead to Vall d'Eina. Your destination is to the right. Go to the other side of the stream and climb up the slope for a few metres to the GR path along which you arrive at a ski slope a few minutes later. Follow this to a signposted junction where you carry straight on along the hiking path beside the stream as far as the Pont de l'Escuder. The two side-valleys of Torrent de Noufonts and Torrent de Noucreus join at this point. Cross the little wooden bridge, then go up to the signpost standing on the right a bit higher up and continue in the direction of Nocreus. The path

Coll de Noucreus – 'pass of the crosses'.

View from Pic de Noufonts of the French mountains.

now runs through the treeless grassy slopes of the valley up a steadily ascending incline. With the partly eroded hillsides the valley pasture is sometimes a bleak spectacle and has few eye-catching reference points. The path begins to go up across the hilly head of the valley and then starts up some wide bends which lead up the scree-covered slope of the col. Below the rocky ridge cross over left to the flat **Coll de Noucreus**, 2775m.

Now continue along the GR11 to the west. It follows the crest of the ridge at first on the left, then on the right, goes past the inconspicuous Pic de Noucreus, 2799m, and then descends quickly to the Coll de Noufonts, 2658m, where a stone shelter has been built. The beautifully shaped Pic de Noufonts rises up further along the line of the ridge and this is what you now head for along the obvious path on the right of the ridge; the appreciably level path which branches off to the right from the pass leads onto the French side to the Coll d'en Bernat. The path now winds up the strenuous incline to the summit rise, briefly steepens up again at the end and reaches the surprisingly flat **Pic de Noufonts**, 2861m, with a summit cross.

Index

A
Agulles d'Amitges 75
Aigüestortes de Morano 50
Alins 88
Andorra 90
Ansovell 124
Àreu 82, 84, 86
Arinsal 92
Arsèguel 124
Artíes 28

B
Baqueira 36, 38
Bellver de Cerdanya 128
Besan 88
Boí 50, 52, 54

C
Cabdella 56
Camí dels Enginyers 148
Camí Vell 144
Canillo 104
Cava 124
Cerbi 76
Cerdanya 116
Circ de Colomèrs 32, 34
Circ de Tristaina 94
Circ dels Pessons 110
Circ dera Artiga 26
Colh de Clòsos 38
Coll d'Ordino 104
Coll de l'Alba 106
Coll de Monestero 64
Coll de Noucreus 152
Coll dels Estanys Forcats 86
Comabona 130
Cornellana 134
Còth der Lac Glaçat 44

E
El Serrat 94, 96, 98, 100
Ermita St. Miquel 88
Es Bòrdes 26
Escaldes 114

Espot 58, 62, 64, 66, 70, 74
Estana 126
Estany Blau 98
Estany d'Estats 82
Estany de Cavallers 54
Estany de Certascan 79
Estany de Gerber 42, 44
Estany de l'Estanyó 102
Estany de la Gola 76
Estany de Lladres 60
Estany de Llebreta 51
Estany de Més Amunt 95
Estany de Monestero 62, 64
Estany de Saburó 57
Estany de Sottlo 82
Estany de St. Maurici 48, 58
Estany de Subenuix 66
Estany del Diable 80
Estany del Mig 94, 96
Estany dels Pessons 110
Estany Gento 56
Estany Llong 52
Estany Negre 92
Estany Negre de Peguera 60
Estanys de Baiau 86
Estanys de Juclar 106
Estanys de Malniu 122
Esterri d'Àneu 76

G
Gorges del Freser 148
Gósol 117

J
Josa 134
Josa de Cadí 117

L
La Rabassa 98, 100, 102
Lac de Mar 24, 28
Lac de Pòdo 34
Lac deth Port de Colomèrs 34
Lac Obago 32, 34
Lacs de Baciver 36

M
Martinet 118, 126, 130
Meranges 120, 122
Mirador de Gresolet 136
Mirador de l'Estany 74
Mirador de St. Maurici 52
Moixeró 116
Montardo d'Aran 30
Montgarri 38
N
Nas 128
Núria 140, 144, 152
O
Ordino 104
Orri 36
P
Parc Nacional d'Aigüestortes 48
Parc Natural Cadí 116
Pas dels Gosolans 130
Pedraforca 136
Penyes Altes de Moixeró 132
Pic d'Amitges 44
Pic d'Escobes 106
Pic de Campirme 80
Pic de Casamanya 104
Pic de Coma Pedrosa 92
Pic de Gargantillar 110
Pic de la Serrera 100
Pic de Monestero 64
Pic de Noufonts 152
Pic de Subenuix 66
Pic de Tristania 96
Pic del Portarró 52
Pica d'Estats 78
Plan de Beret 36, 38
Planell d'Aigüestortes 50, 52
Port de Boet 84
Port de la Bonaigua 44
Pòrt de Ratera 70
Port de Siguer 98
Portarró d'Espot 52
Prat de Cadí 126
Prat de Pierró 59

Puigmal 140
Puigpedrós 120
Q
Queralbs 140, 144, 148, 152
R
Refugi d'Amitges 71, 74
Refugi d'Estany Llong 52
Refugi de Colomèrs 32, 34
Refugi de Colomina 56
Refugi de Coma Pedrosa 92
Refugi de Fontverd 114
Refugi de Juclar 106
Refugi de la Pleta del Prat 80
Refugi de Malniu 120, 122
Refugi de Rialb 98
Refugi de Sorteny 100
Refugi de Vallferrera 82
Refugi del Serrat de les Esposes II 132
Refugi dera Restanca 28
Refugi E. Mallafré 58
Refugi Lluís Estasen 136
Refugi Manelic 151
Refugi Mataró 44
Refugi Prat d'Aguiló 128, 130
Refugi Riu dels Orris 114
Refugi Ventosa i Calvell 54
Riu de Cerdanya 132
S
Salardú 32
Saldes 136
Santuari de Núria 140
Senterada 56
Sierra de Cadí 124
Soldeu 106, 110
St. Maurici 62, 64, 66, 70, 74
St. Miquel 88
T
Taüll 48
Tavascan 80
Tuc de Pèdescauç 38
Tuc de Ratera 70
Tuixén 117

V

Val d'Aran 24
Val dera Artiga de Lin 26
Vall de Cardós 78
Vall de Ferrera 78
Vall de Gerber 42
Vall de la Llosa 118
Vall de Madriu 114
Vall de Monestero 62
Vall de Núria 138
Vall de Sorteny 100
Vall de Subenuix 66
Vall Ferrera 82, 84, 86
Vall Fosca 56
Valle de Sorteny 98
Vulturó 134

CATALAN – ENGLISH GLOSSARY FOR MOUNTAIN WALKERS

Catalan	English	Catalan	English
aigüestortes	meandering streams	gorga, gorgues	gorge
arriu	river	lac, llac	lake
bahns	thermal baths	mas	farmstead
barranc	mountain stream, gorge	mirador	viewing point
		montanha	mountain range
cabana	shepherd's hut, shelter	pas	pass
		pic	summit, peak
cal, can	farmstead	plá, plan, planell	plain
camí, camin	path	pleta	pen, fold
cap	highest point on land, foothill	pont, pontet	bridge
		port, portarró	col, pass
cascada	waterfall	prado, prat	meadow
castell	castle	puig	mountain, hill
cim	peak, summit	rec	stream
circ	cirque, mountain basin	refugì	refuge, mountain hut
clot	depression, furrow, small valley	restanca	dam, reservoir
		ribèra	valley landscape
		riu	stream, river
coll	col, pass	roc	rock, crag
coma	pass	santuari	(pilgrim's) chapel
coret	pass		
embassada	reservoir	serra, serrat	mountains
escales	steps	torrent	mountain stream
estanh, estany	lake		
estret	reservoir	tuc	high peak
font	spring, well	vall	valley

Abbreviations

GR
Sendero de Gran recorrido

long distance path; marked white and red

ARP (**HRP** in France)
Alta Ruta Pirenaica

high mountain trail

PRC
Sendero de Pequeño Recorrido de Catalunya

(Catalonian Pyrenean hiking trail; marked white and yellow or yellow)

Pyrenees 2
French Central ISBN 3-7633-4826-3.

Pyrenees 1
Spanish Central Pyrenees
I.S.B.N 3-7633-4821-2.